Developing Socioemotional Skills for the Philippines' Labor Market

DIRECTIONS IN DEVELOPMENT
Human Development

Developing Socioemotional Skills for the Philippines' Labor Market

Pablo Acosta, Takiko Igarashi, Rosechin Olfindo, and Jan Rutkowski

 WORLD BANK GROUP

Contents

Boxes

Figures

Tables

Acknowledgments

This book was prepared by a team led by Pablo Acosta and that consisted of Takiko Igarashi, Rosechin Olfindo, and Jan Rutkowski. The team gives special thanks to Corinne Bernaldez and Regina Calzado for their outstanding assistance, and to Sean Lothrop for outstanding editorial assistance.

The team would like to thank Harry Patrinos and Gabriel Demombynes, who provided comments and overall guidance; Raja Bentaouet Kattan, Victoria Levin, and Alexandra Valerio, who offered helpful suggestions on the study; and other team members in the Philippines Country Office who, in different ways, contributed to the development of this analysis.

The team also thanks the Australian Department of Foreign Affairs and Trade for providing generous funding to produce this book.

The officials of the Philippine National Economic and Development Authority, the Department of Labor and Employment, the Department of Education, the Commission on Higher Education, and the Technical Education and Skills Development Authority also provided critical information, support, and feedback.

Main Messages

Although the Philippines has achieved remarkable progress in raising the education level of its labor force, the standard proxy for educational attainment—years of formal schooling—is increasingly inadequate as a measure of workforce skills. About one-third of employers report being unable to fill vacancies because of a lack of applicants with requisite skills. Most of these missing skills are not forms of academic knowledge or technical acumen but rather *socioemotional skills*, also known as "noncognitive skills," "soft skills," or "behavioral skills."

Emerging international evidence suggests that socioemotional skills are increasingly crucial to the types of jobs being created by the global economy. Whereas in the past, literacy, numeracy, and various forms of administrative and technical know-how drove gains in worker productivity, structural economic transformation is creating a burgeoning demand for jobs that require skills related to individual behavior, personality, attitude, and mindset. However, governments and educational institutions in many countries, including the Philippines, are only beginning to fully recognize the importance of socioemotional skills and to develop strategies to foster their development.

This study presents new evidence from employer and household surveys on the role of socioemotional skills—as well as more traditional cognitive and technical skills—in the Philippine labor market. The analysis reveals the following:

- The number of Philippine firms that report inadequate workforce skills rose by 30 percent in the past six years alone. Two-thirds of employers report difficulty finding workers with an adequate work ethic or appropriate interpersonal and communications skills.
- Because the education and vocational training sector has been slow to meet the demand for socioemotional skills development, the proportion of firms that provide worker training has doubled over the past six years, and firm-based training increasingly focuses on socioemotional skills.
- In the Philippines, more-educated and employed workers tend to score higher on measures of grit, decision making, agreeableness, and extraversion.
- One standard deviation in socioemotional skills is associated with a 9 percent increase in average daily earnings (approximately US$2). Socioemotional skills

are associated with especially large income increases for women, young workers, less-educated workers, and those employed in the service sector.

- Higher levels of socioemotional skills are also correlated with a greater probability of being employed, having completed secondary education, and pursuing tertiary education.

The Philippines is still at an early stage in terms of its ability to measure and develop socioemotional skills. Studies suggest that primary school is the optimal time for shaping socioemotional skills, but the elementary education curriculum devotes limited resources to their development. Schools continue to be judged solely by students' performance on cognitive achievement tests rather than on soft-skills competencies, and teachers are not appropriately trained to foster the development of those competencies. Developing those should be a priority. Finally, interventions targeting workers entering the labor force can also effectively bolster their socioemotional skills, as well as complementing efforts to improve labor market information and vocational counseling.

Abbreviations

ASEAN	Association of Southeast Asian Nations
DOLE	Department of Labor and Employment
ECED	early childhood education and development
GDP	gross domestic product
IT	information technology
LFS	Labor Force Survey
MAPEH	music, arts, physical education, and health
NCR	National Capital Region
OECD	Organisation for Economic Co-operation and Development
OLS	ordinary least square
PESO	Public Employment Service Office
PIAAC	Programme for the International Assessment of Adult Competencies
PISA	Programme for International Student Assessment
PRACTICE	social problem solving, resilience, achievement motivation, self-control, teamwork, initiative, confidence, and ethics
PSA	Philippines Statistics Authority
SOCCSKSARGEN	South Cotabato, Cotabato, Sultan Kudarat, and Sarangani and General Santos
STEP	Skills Toward Employability and Productivity
SWPBS	Schoolwide Positive Behavior Support
TESDA	Technical Education and Skills Development Authority

Executive Summary

Over the past several decades, the Philippines has dramatically increased the average education level of its labor force (figure ES.1). The country has made especially significant progress in expanding access to secondary and tertiary education. In 1950, more than half of the adult population had no formal education, and less than 5 percent had reached the tertiary level. By 2010, however, 35 percent of the population had completed primary education, 40 percent had completed secondary education, and about 20 percent had completed some tertiary education. In 2010, the literacy rate was estimated at about 98 percent.

Although relatively few jobs in the Philippine economy require highly sophisticated skills, firms that seek to fill these positions often report difficulty finding skilled workers. Only about 5 percent of Philippine workers are employed in positions that require high-order skills, such as professional occupations. Moreover, lack of education does not appear to be a major obstacle to employment, given that about 80 percent of unemployed workers have completed secondary education. However, business surveys show that firms are frequently unable to find workers with the specific types of skills they require.

As the Philippine economy continues to evolve, new jobs are being created that require new sets of skills, but the precise nature and scope of this apparent skills gap remains unclear. In this context, the standard proxy for estimating human capital—years of formal education—is increasingly inadequate. The present study attempts to contribute to a more accurate and comprehensive understanding of labor productivity in the Philippines by directly analyzing the role of skills, in particular socioemotional skills, in the national labor market.

Unlike traditional academic, cognitive, and technical skills, *socioemotional skills*—also known as *soft skills, noncognitive skills,* or *behavioral skills*—reflect the worker's personality, attitude, and mindset. Evidence from developed countries suggests that socioemotional skills are an important component of job performance in a modern economy. This study draws on evidence from employer and household surveys to assess how socioemotional skills, along with more traditional workforce skills, contribute to employment, wages, and productivity in the Philippine labor market.

Figure ES.1 Educational Attainment Has Increased Substantially across Generations, 2010 and 2015

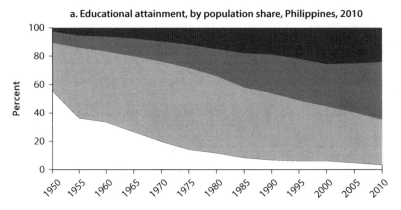

a. Educational attainment, by population share, Philippines, 2010

Source: Barro and Lee 2013.

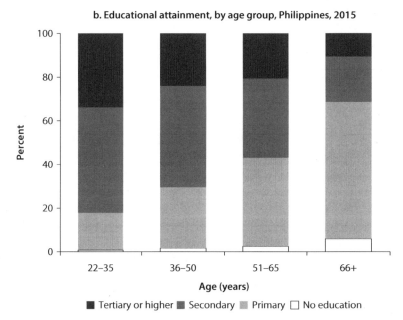

b. Educational attainment, by age group, Philippines, 2015

■ Tertiary or higher ■ Secondary ▨ Primary □ No education

Source: Labor Force Survey 2015; World Bank calculations.

Demand for Socioemotional Skills in the Philippines

A rising share of firms reports having difficulty finding workers with appropriate socioemotional skills (figure ES.2). Between 2009 and 2015, the share of firms that acknowledged having unfilled vacancies because of a lack of qualified candidates increased by about 30 percent. Firms that engage in more complex and sophisticated economic activities are the most likely to cite inadequate workforce skills as a major obstacle to their operations. Among employers trying to hire workers, as many as two-thirds reported challenges finding workers with adequate

Developing Socioemotional Skills for the Philippines' Labor Market
http://dx.doi.org/10.1596/978-1-4648-1191-3

Figure ES.2 Workers with Adequate Socioemotional Skills Are among the Hardest to Find

Source: World Bank Philippines Enterprise Survey 2015; World Bank calculations.
Note: IT = information technology.

work ethics and interpersonal and communication skills, while fewer than one-half reported having difficulty finding workers with adequate technical skills.

Faced with a widening skills gap, Philippine firms increasingly invest in staff training, especially in socioemotional skills. The share of Philippine firms that provide training has doubled in the past six years, and 60 percent of Philippine firms report having provided employee training in the past year, well above the average for the Association of Southeast Asian Nations (ASEAN) member states. Among firms that report having trouble finding workers with appropriate skills, this share rises to 75 percent. More firms train their workers in socioemotional skills than in technical skills, underscoring the country's growing socioemotional skills gap.

Socioemotional Skills and Labor-Market Outcomes

The results of the Skills Toward Employability and Productivity (STEP) survey further illustrate the rising importance of socioemotional skills in the Philippine labor market. The STEP survey assesses the employment-related skills of adults living in urban areas using three modules: (i) a direct evaluation of reading proficiency and related competencies; (ii) self-reported information on personality and behavior; and (iii) an assessment of technical skills that respondents possess or use in their jobs.

In the Philippines, socioemotional skills are positively correlated with employment status and with higher levels of educational attainment. Employed workers have higher grit and decision-making scores and tend to be more agreeable and extraverted than unemployed workers. Respondents with some amount of tertiary education tend to score higher on all socioemotional skill indicators. Young people tend to have lower scores for grit, agreeableness, and decision making. Men and women possess almost identical socioemotional skill sets.

Developing Socioemotional Skills for the Philippines' Labor Market
http://dx.doi.org/10.1596/978-1-4648-1191-3

Greater socioemotional skills tend to correlate with higher earnings (figure ES.3). The STEP survey found that most socioemotional skills are related to labor earnings in a comparable way to that of traditional educational attainment. In the STEP sample, one additional year of education was associated with a 3 percent increase in wages, whereas one standard deviation in socioemotional skills was associated with a 5.6 percent to 9 percent wage increase, or a difference of approximately US$2 per day. Extraversion and openness to new experiences were the socioemotional skills most strongly correlated with increased earning.

Socioemotional skills are most strongly related to higher wages among women and younger workers. Women are more likely to engage in activities that require interpersonal skills. Among male workers, extraversion is the only socioemotional skill that significantly correlates with increased earnings. However, female workers who are more open to new experiences, are extraverted, exhibit strong decision-making power, and possess higher levels of grit and conscientiousness are better rewarded in the labor market. The same is true for younger workers, who drive most of the overall correlation between socioemotional skills and wages.

Socioemotional skills are associated with the greatest wage differential among workers with low educational levels. For less-educated workers, being more extraverted, conscientious, open to new experiences, and agreeable, and exhibiting strong decision-making power, are all associated with greater earnings. However, the same is not the case for more-educated workers. This implies that socioemotional skills tend to substitute for, rather than complement, more traditional cognitive and technical skills, and that they offer a route to higher earnings for workers with limited formal education.

Figure ES.3 All Socioemotional Skills Are Correlated with Higher Labor Income

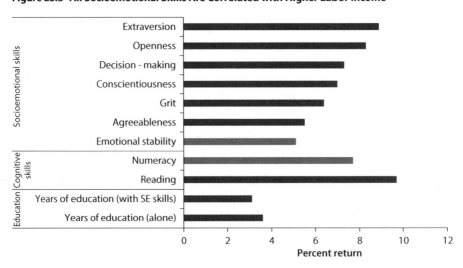

Source: World Bank STEP Household Survey 2015; World Bank calculations.
Note: SE = socioemotional.

Service-sector workers with strong socioemotional skills command a wage premium of about 10 percent. However, socioemotional skills have no significant correlation with wages in the agricultural or manufacturing sectors. This may indicate a selection effect because workers with greater socioemotional skills may pursue employment in fields that value those skills.

Workers with greater socioemotional skills tend to have better employment prospects. A one-standard-deviation increase in socioemotional skills is associated with a 15-percentage-point increase in the probability of being employed. The effect of socioemotional skills on employment is slightly higher among women, older workers, and more-educated workers. By contrast, education level has almost no effect on the probability of being employed.

Finally, socioemotional skills are associated with a higher probability of having completed secondary education and with pursuing tertiary education. Conscientiousness is the skill most closely correlated with a completed secondary education, followed by decision making and grit. Socioemotional skills are also strongly correlated with pursuing—though not necessarily completing—tertiary education.

Education and Skills Development in the Philippines

Along with cognitive and technical skills, the development of socioemotional skills is a vital component of an effective employment and competitiveness strategy. Mainstreaming socioemotional skills into the national educational and training framework will expand employment opportunities, especially for women and younger workers, while helping to close the skills gap reported by employers. Although the Philippines currently lags other developing countries in socioemotional skills development, the international experience yields valuable lessons that could enable the country to rapidly integrate socioemotional skills into the country's national educational and training systems.

The development of socioemotional skills should start at early ages through investing in early childhood education and development (ECED), which needs reform in the Philippines. Along with cognitive development, socioemotional skills development starts in the first 1,000 days of life. Despite the establishment of the Early Childhood Care and Development Act in the year 2000 as a national ECED policy in the Philippines several years ago, implementation is uncoordinated. The Department of Health implements health- and nutrition-related interventions targeting children under two years old; the Department of Social Welfare and Development provides day care and supplemental nutritional support for children three to five years old; and the Department of Education provides schooling and related services from kindergarten to grade 12. Previous efforts to establish a multisector approach to ECED in a decentralized setting yielded highly positive results but were not sustained over time. A renewed focus on coordinating ECED interventions could enhance their effectiveness.

Socioemotional skills development appears to be most effective when targeted to children between the ages of 6 and 11 years. Although children of all ages benefit from socioemotional skills development, intervention during middle childhood appears to have the greatest impact. Children between 6 and 11 years of age possess the neurobiological capacity and psychosocial maturity to effectively practice and learn socioemotional skills. Interventions in middle childhood can also pave the way for the further development of these skills during adolescence. But socioemotional development programs should continue through secondary school and should not be limited to at-risk youth. Schools are the ideal setting in which to teach these skills because the school environment has the greatest influence of any public institution over children and teenagers.

At present, the elementary education curriculum in the Philippines devotes little attention to socioemotional skills (figure ES.4). International experience shows that music, arts, physical education, and health, along with values education, have the greatest impact on socioemotional skills. These subjects stimulate creativity, encourage critical thinking, reward persistence, foster self-motivation, and build self-esteem. However, the Philippine elementary curriculum allocates only 300 minutes per week to these subjects, significantly less than in neighboring countries. Although more time is devoted to these subjects at the secondary level, greater investment at the primary level could increase their effectiveness in developing socioemotional skills. Schools in the Philippines continue to be judged solely by students' performance on cognitive achievement tests, which reduces incentives to teach socioemotional skills; moreover, many teachers are not appropriately trained in socioemotional skills development.

However, socioemotional skills development should augment, not supplant, the teaching of cognitive skills. A recent study on early childhood development in the Philippines focusing on children from kindergarten to second grade revealed that students with high socioemotional skill levels tend to score better on literacy and mathematics tests. In addition, children who have attended preschool tend to score higher on measures of both literacy and socioemotional

Figure ES.4 Philippine Schools Allocate Little Time to Subjects That Foster the Development of Socioemotional Skills

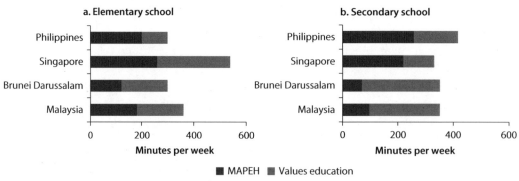

Source: Department of Education and SEAMEO INNOTECH 2012; World Bank calculations.
Note: MAPEH = music, arts, physical education, and health.

skills. Because additional educational interventions (for example, preschool) and specific pedagogical techniques (for example, team-based projects) can foster socioemotional skills development, a curriculum that promotes these skills need not do so at the expense of traditional subjects. The government is currently extending compulsory education from kindergarten through grade 12. Policy makers could leverage the opportunity presented by this initiative by training teachers in pedagogical techniques that promote socioemotional skills development (along with cognitive development) and by integrating regular socioemotional skills testing into the school evaluation process

Apprenticeship programs and other forms of vocational education have also the potential to promote socioemotional skills development, but the effect of these programs in the Philippines has not yet been rigorously evaluated. The Department of Labor and Employment (DOLE) is currently piloting a new youth-employment program known as JobStart, and the Technical Education and Skills Development Authority (TESDA) is implementing a new initiative combining classroom instruction with on-the-job training. Although these interventions have not yet been thoroughly assessed, preliminary data indicate that they have had a positive effect on participant earnings. Further analysis could determine the extent to which these programs promote socioemotional skills development and could reveal opportunities to enhance their effectiveness.

The government is also implementing new instruments to measure skill levels among job seekers, including socioemotional skills, and offering referrals for further skills development. The DOLE is testing new labor market information systems and tools, such as the TalentMap initiative, to directly assess competencies of job seekers. These efforts are expected to facilitate job matching and help narrow the skills gap. Additional workforce surveys and the implementation of international skills assessments (for example, the Programme for International Student Assessment [PISA] and Programme for the International Assessment of Adult Competencies [PIAAC]) could provide policy makers with better information on the socioemotional skills possessed by the Philippine workforce and their effect on employment, wages, and international competitiveness.

Policy Options to Foster Socioemotional Skills

Therefore, the Philippines can build on the impressive reforms taken to date to successfully focus on fostering socioemotional skills by doing the following:

- Reactivate earlier efforts toward a common ECED approach by integrating actions by different agencies toward a common goal (setting up the foundational stages for cognitive and socioemotional development).
- Embed socioemotional skills in the curricula of the extended compulsory education from kindergarten to grade 12 (senior high school) by explicitly stating objectives and targets and by preparing the teachers for effective delivery of content.

- Mainstream socioemotional skills in regular training programs (for example, JobStart, TESDA technical vocational training) after undertaking proper assessment of current delivery performance and impact.
- Invest in monitoring and evaluation tools (for example, TalentMap, regular surveys, participation in international skills assessment efforts such as PISA and PIAAC) to ensure that socioemotional skills are constantly assessed to inform policy formulation.

References

Barro, Robert J., and Johng-Wha Lee. 2013. "A New Data Set of Educational Attainment in the World, 1950–2010." *Journal of Development Economics* 104 (C): 184–98.

Department of Education and SEAMEO INNOTECH (Southeast Asian Ministers of Education Organization Regional Centre for Educational Innovation and Technology). 2012. *K to 12 Education in Southeast Asia: Regional Comparison of the Structure, Content, Organization, and Adequacy of Basic Education.* Quezon City: Philippine Department of Education and Seameo Innotech. http://www.seameo-innotech.org/wp-content /uploads/2014/01/PolRes%20-%20K%20to%2012%20in%20SEA.pdf.

CHAPTER 1

Education and Labor-Market Outcomes in the Philippines

Over the past several decades, the Philippines has greatly increased the education and skill level of its national workforce. In 1950, more than half of the adult population had no formal education, and less than 5 percent had reached the tertiary level. By 2010, educational attainment had dramatically improved: primary completion was nearly universal, and roughly 20 percent of the population had some amount of tertiary education (figure 1.1). The improving trajectory of educational outcomes is evident across age cohorts. Although only 56 percent of workers between the ages of 51 and 64 have completed secondary or tertiary education, the share is 82 percent for workers between the ages of 22 and 35 (figure 1.2).

By the standards of comparable countries, a relatively large share of the Philippine labor force possesses tertiary education. In 2015, about a quarter of the labor force had achieved some degree of tertiary education, well above the average for countries with a similar level of gross domestic product (GDP) per capita (figure 1.3).

However, tertiary completion rates in the Philippines lag those of comparable countries. Although primary completion is nearly universal, only half of primary school graduates proceed to the secondary level, and only half of secondary school graduates proceed to the tertiary level (figure 1.4). Despite the relatively large share of Philippine students who reach the tertiary level, only about half complete their degree. Some students who leave school pursue vocational training or other forms of education, but many others do not. Moreover, quality concerns persist at all levels of the education system.

Consistent with global trends, more-educated workers in the Philippines tend to earn higher wages.[1] About 70 percent of workers who completed tertiary education receive wages in the top 25 percent of the wage distribution (figure 1.5).

Figure 1.1 Distribution of the Population Older Than Age 25, by Educational Attainment, 1950–2010

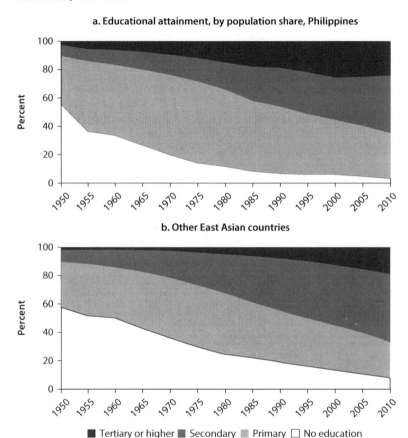

a. Educational attainment, by population share, Philippines

b. Other East Asian countries

■ Tertiary or higher ■ Secondary ▨ Primary ☐ No education

Source: Barro and Lee 2013.
Note: In panel b, the average for China; Hong Kong SAR, China; Taiwan, China; Indonesia; Malaysia; the Republic of Korea; Singapore; and Thailand.

As in other countries, this share declines among workers with less education. The wage differential between workers with completed secondary and completed tertiary education is far larger than the differential between workers with completed primary and completed secondary education. In fact, there is no meaningful difference in wages between workers with incomplete primary, completed primary, and incomplete secondary education. However, there is a large difference between workers with incomplete and completed tertiary education.[2]

Educational attainment is positively correlated with formal employment. About 45 percent of workers with completed tertiary education are employed in the formal sector (figure 1.6). By contrast, only about 10 percent of workers with

Figure 1.2 Distribution of the Labor Force, by Educational Attainment, 2015

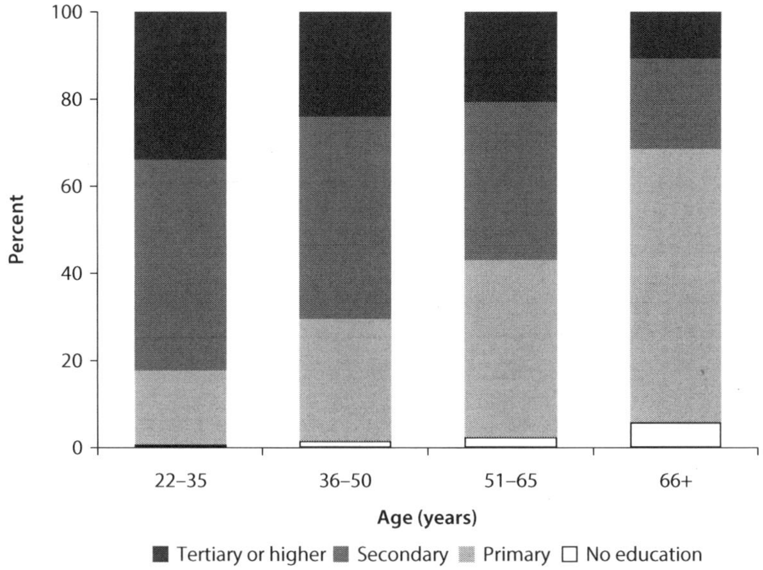

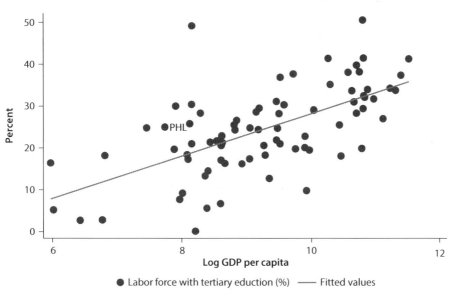

Source: Labor Force Survey 2015; World Bank calculations.

Figure 1.3 Share of the Labor Force with Tertiary Education and Log GDP per Capita

Source: World Development Indicators; World Bank calculations.
Note: GDP = gross domestic product.

Figure 1.4 Gross Enrollment by Education Level, 2012–13

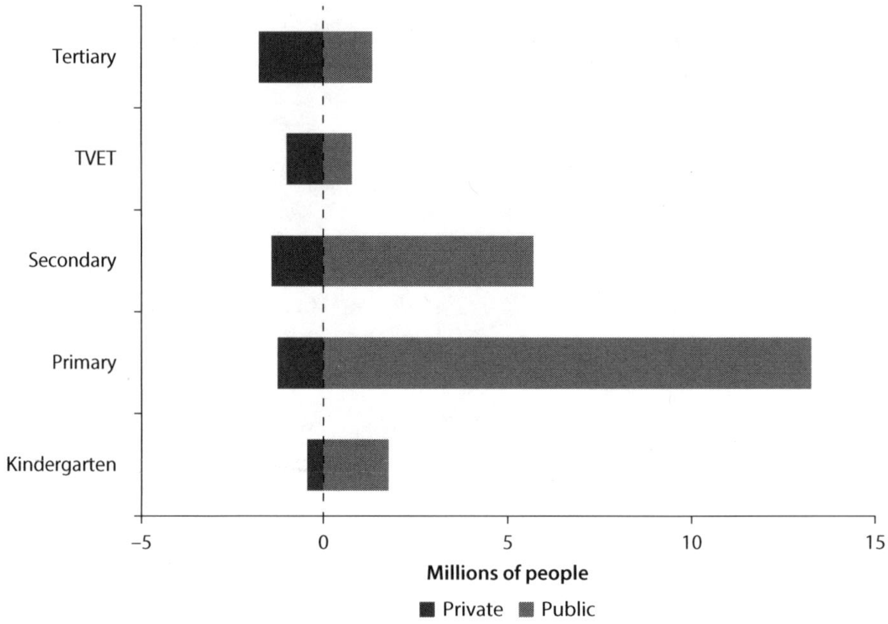

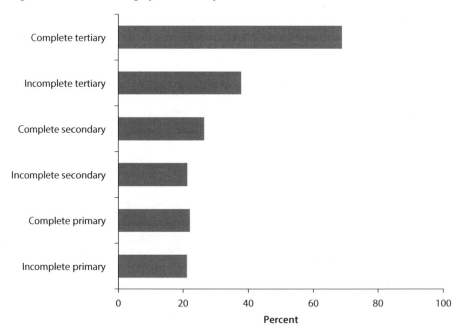

Source: Department of Education; Technical Education and Skills Development Authority; Commission of Higher Education.
Note: TVET = technical and vocational education and training.

Figure 1.5 Incidence of Highly Paid Jobs, by Education Attainment

Source: Labor Force Survey 2015; World Bank calculations.
Note: Highly paid is defined as a wage in the top 25 percent of the wage distribution.

Figure 1.6 Distribution of Wage Workers, by Educational Attainment

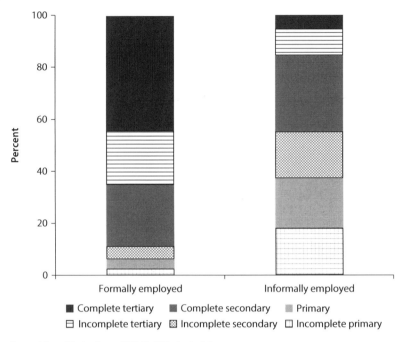

Source: Informal Sector Survey 2008; World Bank calculations.
Note: Formal employment is defined as meeting at least two of the following conditions: (i) the worker is protected from sudden dismissal; (ii) the worker is provided social security; and (iii) the worker has a written contract.

incomplete secondary education or less are employed in the formal sector. Only 5 percent of workers with completed tertiary education are employed in the informal sector, whereas the same is true for more than half of all workers with incomplete secondary education or less. Nevertheless, the correlation between education and formal employment is weaker in the Philippines than in comparable countries.

On the other hand, a significant share of workers with tertiary education are neither employed in occupations that require sophisticated competencies, nor do they receive high wage rates. About 25 percent of workers with completed tertiary education are employed as clerks, and another 17 percent are employed as service workers and unskilled laborers (table 1.1). This type of employment is especially common among workers with incomplete tertiary education. Nevertheless, workers with completed tertiary education receive higher wages than workers with lower levels of educational attainment, even within the same occupations. Wages of managers and professionals who obtained a tertiary degree are about one and a half times higher than the wages of those without a degree. As in other countries, it is unclear to what extent tertiary education increases productivity versus serving as a signaling and screening device.

Developing Socioemotional Skills for the Philippines' Labor Market
http://dx.doi.org/10.1596/978-1-4648-1191-3

Table 1.1 Average Wages and Distribution of Workers by Occupation and Education, 2015

Occupation	Completed secondary		Incomplete tertiary		Completed tertiary	
	Average wages	Employed (% distribution)	Average wages	Employed (% distribution)	Average wages	Employed (% distribution)
Managers	595	2	577	4	913	15
Professionals	527	<1	1,205	<1	836	26
Technicians	416	3	406	5	589	10
Clerks	403	4	467	14	553	24
Operators	385	12	386	11	503	4
Craftsmen	362	22	394	16	413	4
Service and sales workers	322	21	358	27	392	12
Unskilled laborers	267	36	280	23	319	5
Farmers and fishermen	353	<1	..	..	..	..
Other occupations	180	<1	..	..	..	..
All workers	331	100.0	376	100	645	100

Source: Labor Force Survey 2015; World Bank calculations.
Note: Wages are expressed in pesos per day. .. = Negligible.

Similarly, workers with higher levels of educational attainment report longer delays in finding employment and are more likely to be unemployed, suggesting a mismatch between supply and demand for workers in skill-intensive occupations. Workers with completed tertiary education spend an average of 5.5 weeks searching for a job, far longer than the average time spent by workers with lower education levels (table 1.2). Workers with completed tertiary education and previous work experience face longer job-search durations than workers with completed tertiary education who are entering the labor market for the first time. Unemployment rates also increase with education level. About 80 percent of unemployed workers have completed secondary education or higher. Although highly educated workers may have higher reservation wages, face larger differences in wage rates between jobs, and have greater resources to continue an extended job search, the correlation between education and job-search time may indicate a mismatch between the skills possessed by highly educated workers and those demanded by the labor market.

Indeed, many job vacancies go unfilled because of a lack of qualified applicants, providing further evidence of a skills mismatch. About one-third of employers reported having unfilled vacancies because of a shortage of applicants with the necessary skillset (figure 1.7).[3] Moreover, inadequate experience among applicants and receiving few applications for the advertised position are among the most frequently cited reasons for unfilled vacancies.

Poor educational quality may contribute to this apparent skills mismatch. Many tertiary graduates do not pass the license examinations required for professional occupations (figure 1.8). Licensed professionals must meet the standards established by the boards of professional associations. On average,

Table 1.2 Distribution of Workers, by Education Level

Education level	Length of job search (no. of weeks)		Unemployment	
	With experience	New entrants	Rate (%)[a]	Distribution (%)
Incomplete elementary	3.5	4.1	2.5	5.6
Complete elementary	3.1	4.3	2.8	5.9
Incomplete secondary	4.0	2.8	5.9	11.8
Complete secondary	4.1	4.3	8.0	42.0
Incomplete tertiary	4.2	3.2	8.5	12.5
Complete tertiary and above	5.5	3.5	8.5	22.2
All workers	100	100	6.4	100

Source: Labor Force Survey 2015; World Bank calculations.
a. Number of unemployed workers relative to the labor force by education level.

Figure 1.7 Firms' Most Frequently Cited Reasons for Unfilled Vacancies

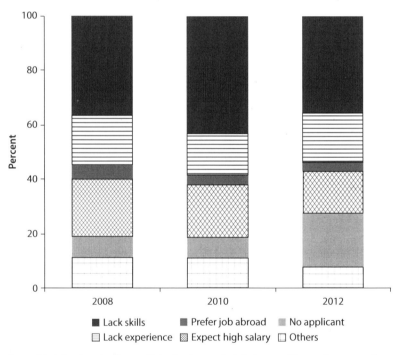

Source: Calculations based on Bureau of Labor Employment Statistics Integrated Surveys, Department of Labor and Employment.

only 60 percent of graduates pass the license examinations, suggesting that tertiary education may leave many students unprepared to meet the demands of the job market.

Thus, this combined evidence suggests that the ongoing structural transformation of the Philippine economy is creating a demand for new skills that are not yet adequately supplied by the labor force. Moreover, the standard proxy for workforce skills—years of education—is an increasingly inadequate metric. As shown in greater detail in the next chapter, although traditional cognitive and technical skills remain closely correlated with employment and wage rates, mounting evidence in developed countries suggests that so-called socioemotional skills play an increasingly important role in the modern labor market (box 1.1).

Despite mounting evidence of the value of socioemotional skills, workforce surveys do not fully capture this dimension of human capital. A lack of data leaves policy makers ill-equipped to develop education and training strategies that will effectively meet the demands of the labor market. In this context,

Figure 1.8 Pass Rate for License Examinations, by Discipline

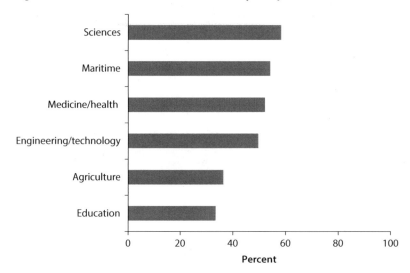

Source: Commission of Higher Education.

Box 1.1 Understanding Socioemotional Skills

Socioemotional skills, also known as "soft skills" or "noncognitive skills," are related to individual behavior, personality, attitude, and mindset. The concept of socioemotional skills was developed in the literature on educational psychology. Payton et al. (2008) and Durlak et al. (2011) define *socioemotional skills* as the relative capacity of individuals to (i) recognize and manage their emotions, (ii) cope successfully with conflict, (iii) navigate interpersonal problem solving, (iv) understand and show empathy for others, (v) establish and maintain positive relationships, (vi) make ethical and safe choices, (vii) contribute constructively to their community, and (viii) set and achieve positive goals. They define *socioemotional learning* as the process of acquiring and applying this set of competencies. Although socioemotional skills differ from

box continues next page

Box 1.1 Understanding Socioemotional Skills *(continued)*

traditional measures of intelligence, their tendency to interact with intelligence must be taken into consideration when measuring outcomes and inferring causal relationships.

Socioemotional skills are part of a constellation of related concepts with overlapping definitions. Although the literature uses a range of terms to describe socioemotional skills, Heckman and Kautz (2013) suggest that all the terms presented in table B1.1.1 below refer to the same concept and can be used interchangeably. Duckworth and Yeager (2015, page 239) concur, stating that "all of the … terms refer to the same conceptual space, even if connotations differ." They note that all of these terms describe skills that are "(a) conceptually independent from cognitive ability, (b) generally accepted as beneficial to the student and to others in society, (c) relatively rank-order stable over time in the absence of exogenous forces … (d) potentially responsive to intervention, and (e) dependent on situational factors for their expression."

Table B1.1.1 Socioemotional Skills and Related Concepts

Term	Definition
Socioemotional skills	Social, emotional, behavioral, attitudinal, and personality-related competencies
Soft skills	Creativity, listening skills, problem solving, creative thinking, leadership, teamwork, and ability to work independently
Noncognitive skills	Skills not captured by cognitive tests
Character skills	Qualities needed to realize individual potential by developing talents, working hard, and achieving goals
Personality qualities	Openness, conscientiousness, extraversion, agreeableness, and emotional stability
21st-century skills	Skills involving (i) innovation and creativity, critical thinking and problem solving, and communication and collaboration; (ii) facility with information, media, and technology, including the ability to access, evaluate, use, and manage information, analyze media, create media products, and apply technology effectively; (iii) life and career skills such as flexibility and adaptability, initiative and self-direction, social and cross-cultural skills, productivity and accountability, and leadership and responsibility
Life skills	Skills related to (i) the capacity to analyze and use information, (ii) the development of personal agency, and (iii) communication and interpersonal interaction.

Source: Puerta et al. 2016.

---

this study presents new evidence from both employer and household surveys regarding the state of workforce skills in the Philippine economy, with a focus on the role of socioemotional skills. The study attempts to determine which socioemotional skills Philippine employers value most, which skills the labor force possesses, and which skills exhibit the largest degree of unfulfilled demand. It concludes by assessing policy options for bolstering socioemotional skills in the Philippines and identifying the key features of a successful strategy for developing those skills.

Developing Socioemotional Skills for the Philippines' Labor Market
http://dx.doi.org/10.1596/978-1-4648-1191-3

Notes

1. For a comprehensive analysis of the Philippine labor market, see World Bank (2013, 2016).

2. Previous studies in the Philippines have shown that education is the most important contributor to earnings differentials, and that the wage premium generated by education increases with education level (Tan and Paqueo 1989; Gerochi 2002; Schady 2003; Luo and Terada 2009). An earlier study found that the expansion of education services in the 1980s did not diminish the profitability of education investments (Hossain and Psacharopoulos 1994). More recent studies have revealed that the returns to education remain positive, implying that further investment in education would be justified by the resulting economic gains (di Gropello, Tan, and Tandon 2010; Albert et al. 2011).

3. The Bureau of Labor Employment Statistics Integrated Survey (BITS) is a nationwide survey of firms with at least 20 workers.

References

Albert, Jose Ramon G., Rafaelita M. Aldaba, Roehlano M. Briones, Danilo C. Israel, Gilberto M. Llanto, Erlinda M. Medalla,Adoracion M. Navarro, Aniceto C. Orbeta, Vincente B. Paqueo, Celia M. Reyes, Aubrey D. Tabuga, and Josef T. Yap. 2011. "Education for Development." *Philippine Institute for Development Studies 2011 Economic Policy Monitor*. Philippines Institute for Development Studies, Makati City, Philippines. https://dirp3.pids.gov.ph/ris/books/pidsbk12-epm2011.pdf.

Barro, Robert J., and Johng-Wha Lee. 2013. "A New Data Set of Educational Attainment in the World, 1950–2010." *Journal of Development Economics* 104 (C): 184–98.

di Gropello, Emanuela, Hong Tan, and Prateek Tandon. 2010. *Skills for the Labor Market in the Philippines*. Directions in Development Series. Washington, DC: World Bank.

Duckworth, Angela L., and David Scott Yaeger. 2015. "Measurement Matters: Assessing Personal Qualities Other than Cognitive Ability for Educational Purposes." *Educational Researcher* 44 (4): 237–51.

Durlak, Joseph A., Roger P. Weissberg, Allison B. Dymnicki, Rebecca D. Taylor, and Kriston B. Schellinger. 2011. "The Impact of Enhancing Students' Social and Emotional Learning: A Meta-Analysis of School-Based Universal Interventions." *Child Development* 82 (1): 405–32.

Gerochi, Hope A. 2002. "Returns to Education in the Philippines." *The Philippine Review of Economics* 39 (2): 37–72.

Heckman, James J., and Tim Kautz. 2013. "Fostering and Measuring Skills: Interventions that Improve Character and Cognition." NBER Working Paper 19656, National Bureau of Economic Research, Cambridge, MA.

Hossain, Shaikh I., and George Psacharopoulos. 1994. "The Profitability of School Investments in an Educationally Advanced Developing Country." *International Journal of Educational Development* 14 (1): 35–42.

Luo, Xubei, and Takanobu Terada. 2009. "Education and Wage Differentials in the Philippines." Policy Research Working Paper 5120, World Bank, Washington, DC.

Payton, John, Roger P. Weissberg, Joseph A. Durlak, Allison B. Dymnicki, Rebecca D. Taylor, Kriston B. Schellinger, and Molly Pachan. 2008. "The Positive Impact of Social and Emotional Learning for Kindergarten to Eighth-Grade Students: Findings from Three Scientific Reviews—Technical Report." Collaborative for Academic, Social, and Emotional Learning, Chicago, IL.

Puerta, Sanchez, Maria Laura, Alexandria Valerio, and Marcela Gutierrez Bernal. 2016. *Taking Stock of Programs to Develop Socioemotional Skills:* A Systematic Review of Program Evidence.

Directions in Development Series. Washington, DC: World Bank.

Schady, Norbert R. 2003. "Convexity and Sheepskin Effects in the Human Capital Earnings Function: Recent Evidence for Filipino Men." *Oxford Bulletin of Economics and Statistics* 65 (2): 171–96.

Tan, Jee-Peng, and Vicente B. Paqueo. 1989. "The Economic Returns to Education in the Philippines." *International Journal of Educational Development* 9 (3): 243–50.

World Bank. 2013. "Philippine Development Report: Creating More and Better Jobs." Report No. ACS5842. World Bank, Washington, DC.

———. 2016. "Republic of the Philippines Labor Market Review: Employment and Poverty in the Philippines." World Bank, Washington, DC.

CHAPTER 2

Demand for Socioemotional Skills in the Philippine Labor Market

Introduction

This chapter presents evidence of the latest Philippines Enterprise Survey carried out by the World Bank in 2015. It finds that, for the majority of Philippine firms, skills are not the most critical concern (in relation to others such as corruption or taxes), but a growing concern. Also, medium-size, modern, and growing firms tend to report such skills shortages more frequently. The policy challenge is, thus, to address the skill needs of these firms to support modernization and growth of the Philippine economy.

Demand for Skills among Philippine Firms

Although a lack of adequate workforce skills is not the challenge most frequently cited by Philippine firms, there is evidence of a widening skills mismatch. Only 10 percent of Philippine firms identify inadequate workforce education as a critical obstacle to doing business, a smaller share than in most Association of Southeast Asian Nations (ASEAN) member states (figures 2.1 and 2.2). Inadequate workforce skills rank 12th out of 16 obstacles to doing business identified by Philippine firms, and the most frequently cited were corruption, tax rates, and competition from the informal sector (figure 2.3). However, the share of firms that cite inadequate workforce skills as a major challenge is increasing over time (table 2.1).

Between 2009 and 2015, the number of firms citing inadequate workforce skills as a major obstacle to doing business rose by 30 percent. This large increase, albeit from a low base, was driven by firms in the service sector. Because the share of services in the Philippine economy is rising over time, this skills gap is likely to widen. Correlations between reported skills shortages and other firm-level characteristics appear to confirm that this skills gap is likely to widen because rapidly growing firms working in innovative sectors and located in large urban areas are the most likely to report difficulty finding workers with the necessary skills.

Figure 2.1 Extent to Which Philippine Firms Perceive Inadequate Workforce Skills as an Obstacle to Doing Business in the Philippines

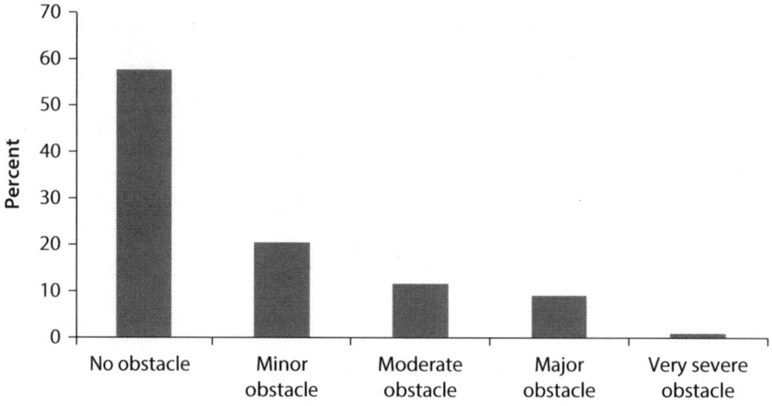

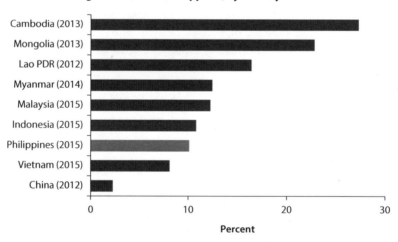

Source: World Bank Enterprise Surveys, various years; calculations based on World Bank Enterprise Surveys.

Figure 2.2 Percentage of Firms that Identify Inadequate Skills as a Major Obstacle to Doing Business in the Philippines, by Country

Source: World Bank Enterprise Surveys, various years; calculations based on World Bank Enterprise Surveys.

Rapidly growing firms are most likely to report skills shortages. Firms that are in the process of recruiting new workers are twice as likely as nonrecruiting firms to cite problems with inadequate workforce skills (figure 2.4). Firms that are expanding are also substantially more likely to report skills shortages than firms that are stagnant or contracting (figure 2.5). Although this correlation may be partially explained by sample selection—because skills shortages are likely to present a more immediate and visible challenge for firms in the process of recruiting new workers—the strength of the correlation across multiple metrics of firm expansion

http://dx.doi.org/10.1596/978-1-4648-1191-3

Figure 2.3 Major Obstacles to Doing Business Identified by Firms in the Philippines

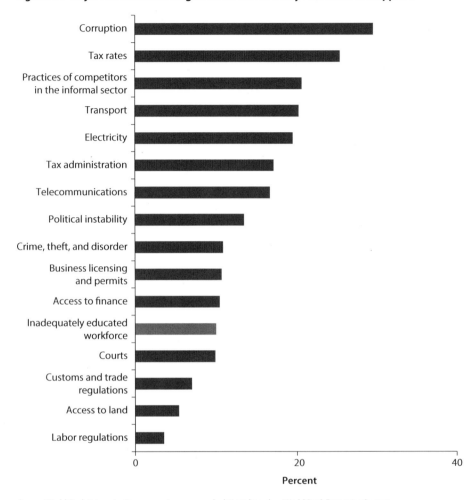

Source: World Bank Enterprise Surveys, various years; calculations based on World Bank Enterprise Surveys.

Table 2.1 Percentage of Firms Identifying Inadequate Skills as a Major Obstacle to Doing Business in the Philippines, 2009 and 2015

	2009 (%)	2015 (%)	Increase (percentage points)
All firms	7.8	10.1	**2.3**
Manufacturing	6.7	7.3	0.6
Services	8.2	11.0	**2.8**

Source: World Bank Enterprise Surveys 2009, 2015; World Bank calculations.

presents compelling evidence that inadequate workforce skills tend to be especially problematic for the most dynamic firms in the Philippine economy.

Inadequate workforce skills are also a major obstacle for innovative firms. *Innovative firms* are defined as those that introduced new or significantly improved products or services, or adopted new production methods, during the

Figure 2.4 Share of Firms Citing Inadequate Skills as a Major Obstacle to Doing Business in the Philippines, by Hiring Status

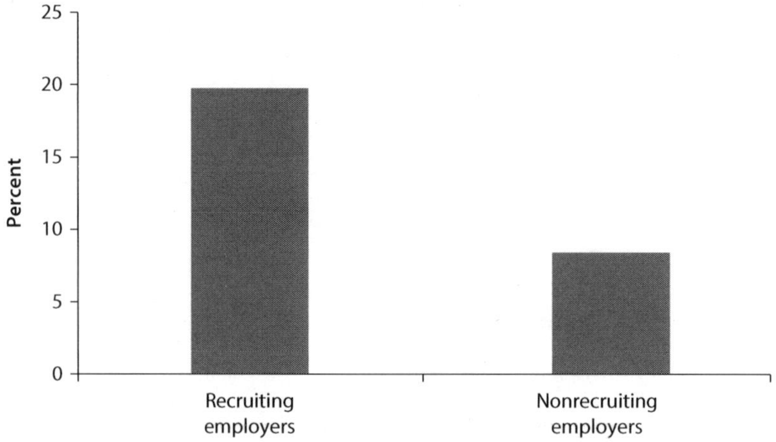

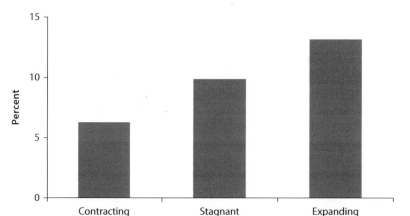

Source: World Bank Enterprise Surveys 2015; World Bank calculations.

Figure 2.5 Share of Firms Citing Inadequate Skills as a Major Obstacle to Doing Business in the Philippines, by Firm Growth Trajectory

Source: World Bank Enterprise Surveys 2015; World Bank calculations.

past three years. Innovative firms are six times more likely to be dissatisfied with workforce education than traditional firms (figure 2.6). One in five innovative firms identifies inadequate workforce education as a major constraint to doing business, and innovative firms represent more than 80 percent of all firms that consider inadequate workforce skills to be a major constraint.

Medium-size service-sector firms located in large cities are the most likely to identify inadequate workforce skills as an obstacle to doing business. Medium-size firms—defined as firms employing 20–99 workers—are twice as likely as smaller firms to cite inadequate workforce skills as a major challenge (figure 2.7). Medium-size firms may face the most acute skills shortage because, although

Figure 2.6 Share of Firms Citing Inadequate Skills as a Major Obstacle to Doing Business in the Philippines, by Propensity to Innovate

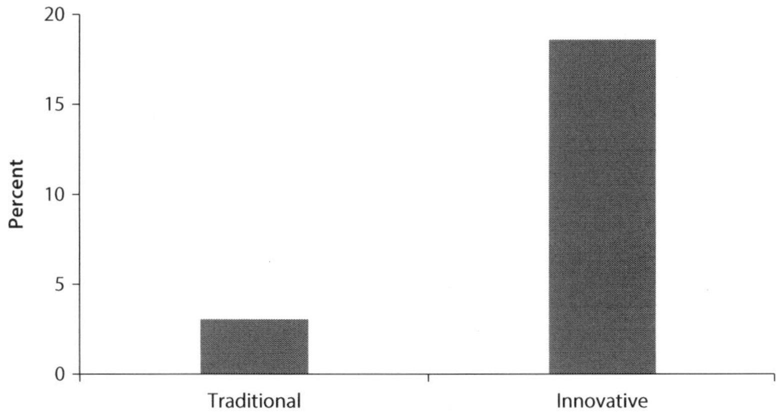

Source: World Bank Enterprise Surveys 2015; World Bank calculations.

Figure 2.7 Share of Firms Citing Inadequate Skills as a Major Obstacle to Doing Business in the Philippines, by Firm Size

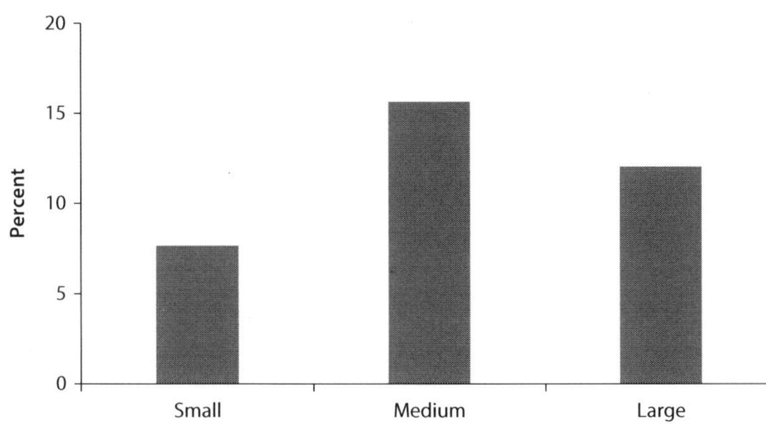

Source: World Bank Enterprise Surveys 2015; World Bank calculations.

their operations are more skill-intensive than those of smaller firms, they lack the recruiting resources of larger firms. Eleven percent of service-sector firms and 7 percent of manufacturing firms report experiencing a skills shortage.[1] Reported skills shortages are especially acute among firms in Metro Manila, and firms located in cities with more than 1 million inhabitants are also two and a half to three times more likely to express dissatisfaction with workforce skills than firms in smaller cities (figure 2.8). However, firms located in towns with fewer than 50,000 inhabitants also frequently report being unable to find workers with adequate skills. Whereas in large cities the skills shortage is probably driven by a relatively high demand for skilled labor, in small towns the problem is likely due

Developing Socioemotional Skills for the Philippines' Labor Market
http://dx.doi.org/10.1596/978-1-4648-1191-3

Figure 2.8 Share of Firms Citing Inadequate Skills as a Major Obstacle to Doing Business in the Philippines, by Firm Location

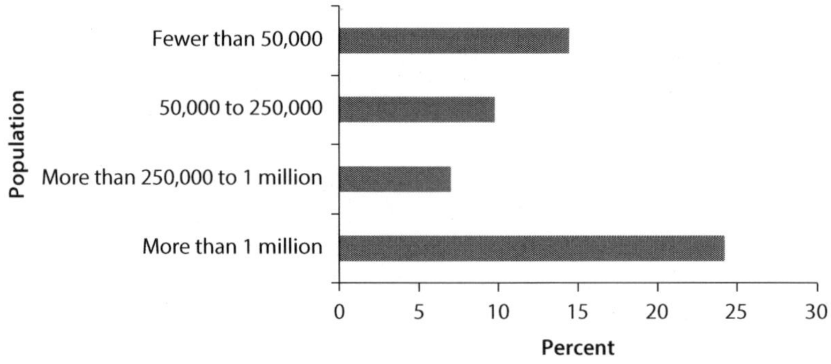

Source: World Bank Enterprise Surveys 2015; World Bank calculations.

to low supply: small towns not only have smaller pools of workers but also often lose a portion of their skilled labor as workers migrate to larger cities.[2]

Propensity to innovate is the firm-level characteristic most strongly associated with reported skills shortages. Regression analysis reveals that having a propensity to innovate, operating in the service sector, and being based in a large city are all independently correlated with having difficulty finding skilled workers.[3] However, the correlation with propensity to innovate is the most significant and robust across specifications.

Hiring Constraints among Philippine Firms

Among firms that report difficulty hiring workers, the most frequently cited reason is inadequate job skills, followed by high employee wage expectations and lack of applicants (figure 2.9). Although the large share of firms that report inadequate workforce skills clearly indicates a skills shortage, high wage expectations and a lack of applicants may also be indirect consequences of a skills shortage.[4] Applicants may reject wage offers because they have skills that are in high demand, and the small number of applicants may indicate that very few workers have skills that match the job description.

The specific skills that employers most value when hiring, but are unable to find, are primarily socioemotional skills. These include interpersonal and communication skills and a strong work ethic (figure 2.10). Firms also report, but less frequently, challenges finding workers with the right technical and vocational skills. Among firms that were attempting to hire workers, two-thirds reported that it was difficult to find workers with adequate work ethics, while less than one-half reported it was difficult to find workers with adequate technical skills.

The apparent socioemotional skills deficit implies that the Philippine education system should place greater emphasis on the development of these skills to equip students with the competencies demanded by the labor market. A greater endowment of socioemotional skills would facilitate job matching and support

Figure 2.9 Challenges Cited by Philippine Firms Unable to Fill Vacancies

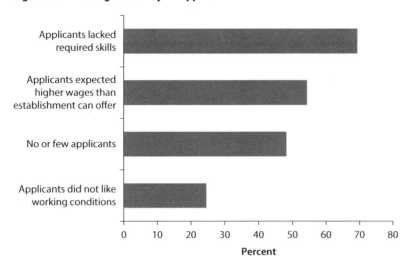

Source: World Bank Philippine Enterprise Survey 2015; World Bank calculations.

Figure 2.10 Skills that Philippine Firms Report Having Difficulty Acquiring Applicants to Fulfill

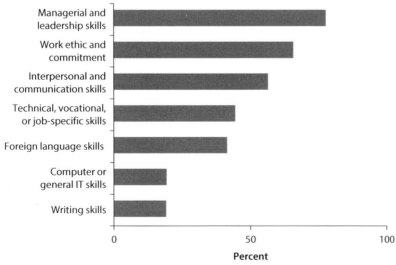

Source: World Bank Philippine Enterprise Survey 2015; World Bank calculations.
Note: IT = information technology.

productivity growth. Recent evidence of a widening socioemotional skills gap is broadly consistent with previous findings for the Philippines (box 2.1) and international experience (box 2.2).

Recent data from the Enterprise Surveys corroborate the conclusion of previous analyses, which suggest that workers are often hired for their technical skills

Box 2.1 Findings from Previous World Bank Research

Earlier studies have found that skills demand in the Philippines is driven by changes in output and employment structure, openness to new technology, and the pressures of international competition (di Gropello, Tan, and Tandon 2010), and that Philippine employers require a combination of job-specific and generic skills, including socioemotional skills. Philippine employers were found to value the capacity to work and solve problems independently, communicate effectively, engage in teamwork, manage time effectively, and apply business theory in practical environments (figure B2.1.1). However, many of these essential skills appeared to be in short supply, and the Philippine labor market had a larger number of vacancies for skilled positions than labor markets elsewhere in the region. Finding skilled workers took an average of five weeks in the Philippines, versus just two and a half weeks in Vietnam and three weeks in both Indonesia and the Republic of Korea. Almost 70 percent of Philippine workers were trained by firms, compared to an average of 60 percent in the region and 54 percent worldwide (World Bank 2009).

Therefore, the findings of this present study confirm the conclusions of previous analytical work.

Figure B2.1.1 Skills Demanded by Employers in the Philippines, by Occupation

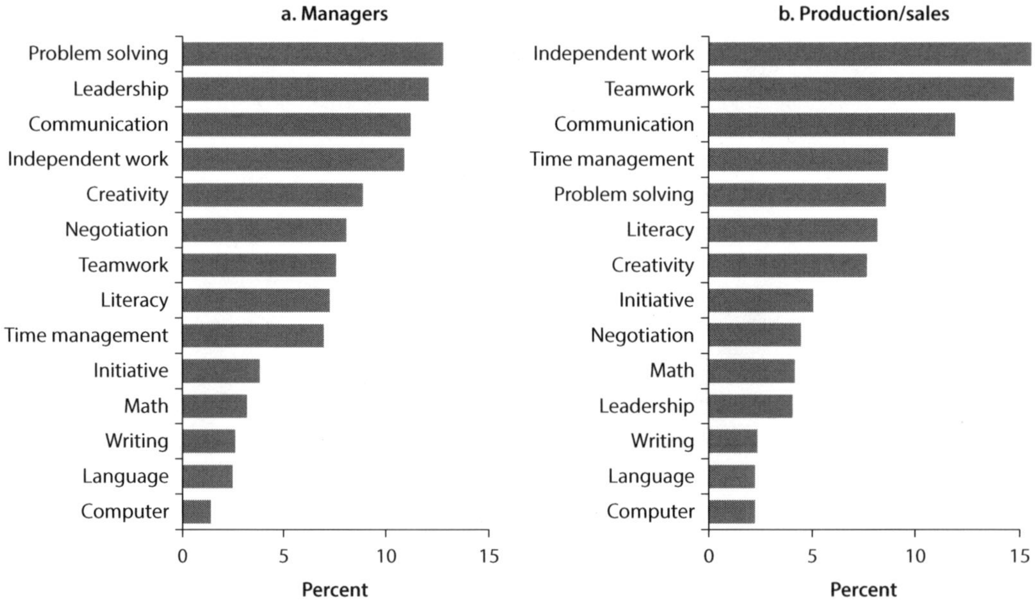

Source: Di Gropello, Tan, and Tandon 2010.

Box 2.2 Global Demand for Workforce Skills

There is growing evidence that the demand for socioemotional skills is rising in both developing and developed countries. In a 2012 survey, employers in Argentina, Brazil, and Chile all ranked socioemotional skills as the most desired skill type, followed by cognitive skills and technical skills (Busso et al. 2012). A meta-analysis of 28 studies revealed remarkable consistency in the skills demanded by employers worldwide (Cunningham and Villaseñor 2014).[a] Although employers value all skill sets, demand for socioemotional skills and higher-order cognitive skills is consistently greater than demand for basic cognitive skills and technical skills. More than three-quarters of the studies found that the skill most valued by employers was a socioemotional skill, and half identified a socioemotional skill among the top five most-valued skills. Highly valued socioemotional skills include work ethic, interpersonal skills, honesty, teamwork, attitude, integrity, punctuality, and responsibility. And among the almost 30 percent of studies that identified a higher-order cognitive skill among the top five skills, critical thinking, efficiency, and leadership (which some associate with socioemotional skills) were the most highly valued. These results are robust across economies of varying sizes and levels of development, as well as sector, export orientation, and occupation type. The high value employers place on socioemotional and higher-order cognitive skills may reflect a decline in the relative number of jobs that require manual labor and an increase in the relative number of jobs that require nonroutine analysis and independent reasoning (Aedo et al. 2013).

a. This meta-analysis classifies over 140 skills from the 28 studies into four groups: socioemotional, lower-order cognitive, higher-order cognitive, and technical.

---

but fired for their unsatisfactory socioemotional skills. Of firms, 27 percent reported having fired workers during the two years preceding the survey because of either a lack of required technical skills or poor job performance, which can be interpreted as a lack of essential socioemotional skills. Twenty-five percent of firms reported firing workers for poor performance, whereas 14 percent reported firing workers for inadequate technical skills.[5]

The data indicate that innovative firms are much more likely to fire workers than traditional firms and are especially prone to fire workers for poor performance. Innovative firms are twice as likely as traditional firms to fire workers for lack of technical skills but three times as likely to fire for poor performance (figure 2.11). The tendency of innovative firms to fire workers for poor performance reinforces the conclusion that these firms value socioemotional skills more highly than traditional firms.

Training Practices among Philippine Firms

Not surprisingly, Philippine firms are more likely to invest in workforce training than firms in other countries. A growing number of Philippine firms is attempting to bridge the skills gap by providing formal training to their workers. Currently, about 60 percent of Philippine firms provide formal training, a much larger share than in most other ASEAN countries (figure 2.12).[6] For example,

Figure 2.11 Share of Philippine Firms That Fired Workers over the Past Two Years for Lack of Required Skills or Poor Performance, by Firm Propensity to Innovate

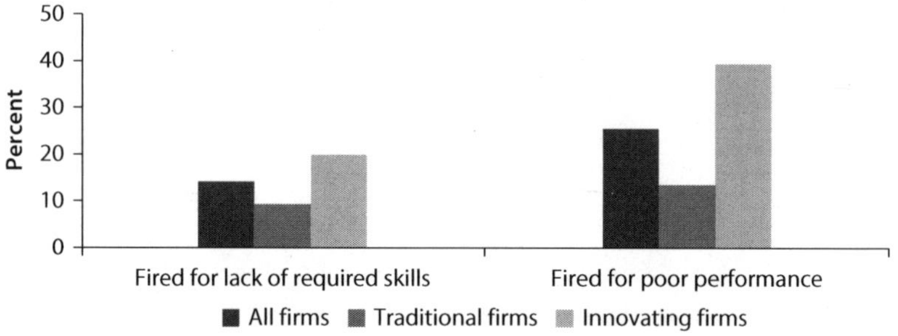

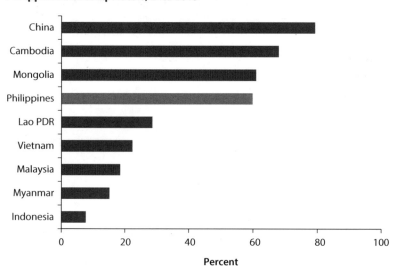

Source: World Bank Philippine Enterprise Survey 2015; World Bank calculations.

Figure 2.12 Share of Firms Providing Formal Employee Training, Philippines and Comparators, circa 2015

Source: World Bank Enterprise Surveys; World Bank calculations.

only about 20 percent of firms in Malaysia and Vietnam train their workers. Moreover, the share of Philippine firms that provide training doubled between 2009 and 2015. Although further research could shed light on the types of training offered and the specific reasons firms choose to train their workers, the rising prevalence of employer training presents strong evidence of a widening skills gap.

Firms that report inadequate workforce skills as an obstacle to doing business are more likely to provide training. A full 75 percent of firms that reported difficulty finding appropriately skilled workers provided training, compared with less than 60 percent of firms that did not report similar challenges finding skilled workers. This finding reinforces the conclusion that Philippine firms face a widening skills gap, and it highlights the role firms play in upskilling the formal labor force. The prevalence of training indicates that many firms can find workers with the necessary foundational skills and then train those workers in more specific skills. However, it is not clear how the efficiency of firm-based training compares to that of public investment in workforce skills.

Young, large, and innovative firms in the services sector are the most likely to train their employees. The incidence of firm-based training declines with firm age (figure 2.13). Almost 70 percent of recently established firms provide training, compared with just over 50 percent of firms established more than 20 years ago. However, propensity to innovate is the firm-level characteristic most closely correlated with training (table 2.2). Seventy percent of innovative firms provide

Figure 2.13 Share of Firms That Provide Training in the Philippines, by Firm Age

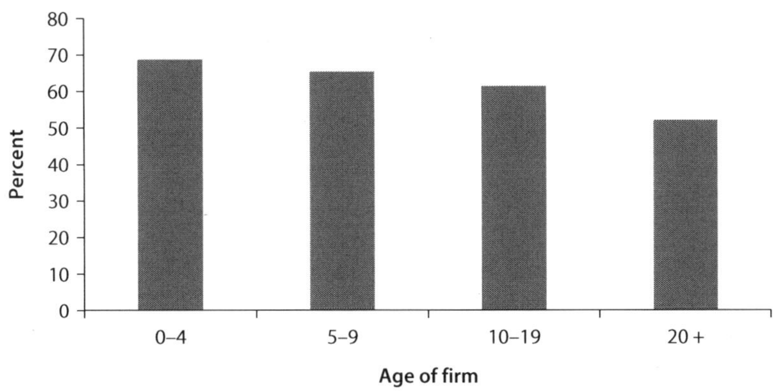

Source: World Bank Philippine Enterprise Survey 2015; World Bank calculations.

Table 2.2 Share of Firms That Provide Training, by Firm Characteristics

Firm characteristic	Firms that provide training (%)
Size	
Small	59
Medium	59
Large	80
Sector	
Services	64
Manufacturing	48
Innovation status	
Innovative	71
Traditional	51
Growth status	
Expanding (employment)	62
Stagnant or contracting	58
Export status	
Exporting	65
Not exporting	59

Source: World Bank Enterprise Surveys 2015; World Bank calculations.

training, compared to just 50 percent of traditional firms. Last, 64 percent of service-sector firms provide training, versus 48 percent of manufacturing firms. Larger firms are also more likely to provide training. Other factors, such as firm growth rates and export orientation, had no statistically significant correlation with firms' propensity to provide training.

Regression analysis reveals that only three factors have an independent and statistically significant effect on whether firms provide training: (i) propensity to innovate, (ii) firm size, and (iii) economic sector.[7] After controlling for these factors, the effect of firm age disappears. As younger firms tend to be innovative and operate in the service sector, firm age may be a marker only for these two underlying factors. Large firms are more likely to have the necessary resources to provide training, and they may tend to engage in more complex forms of production that require more specific and diverse sets of skills. The fact that service-sector firms provide training more frequently than manufacturing firms is specific to the Philippines. It likely reflects both the rising importance of more sophisticated services in the Philippine economy and the predominantly traditional nature of Philippine manufacturing.

The correlation between innovation and training at the firm level underscores the economic consequences of the skills gap. The introduction of new products or technologies often requires new workforce skills. The absence of adequately trained workers can slow the economy's technological evolution and structural transformation. Enhancing the national education and training system could alleviate the training costs borne by innovative firms and thereby encourage the growth of new industries and sectors.

Correlations between firm training and indicators of technological sophistication further support the contention that training is most common among cutting-edge firms. Smaller traditional firms operating in less technologically advanced economic sectors are the least likely to provide training. For example, 68 percent of firms that do not provide training also do not have a website, whereas 66 percent of firms that do provide training also have a website.

More firms train their workers in socioemotional skills than in technical skills. This is consistent with the finding that Philippine firms tend to face greater difficulty finding employees with the appropriate socioemotional skills. Of firms, 46 percent train workers primarily in socioemotional skills, whereas 30 percent train them in technical or vocational skills (figure 2.14). Most technical training programs focus on computer and information technology skills, whereas most socioemotional training programs focus on work ethics (22 percent) and interpersonal and communication skills (18 percent). Technical and vocational training is undoubtedly indispensable to the productivity and competitiveness of many Philippine firms, but training in socioemotional skills addresses a wider skills deficit with critical economy-wide ramifications. The growing importance of firm-based training in socioemotional skills underscores the extent to which the Philippine educational system is not evolving swiftly enough to meet the demands of the labor market.

Figure 2.14 Share of Philippine Firm Training Programs, by Primary Focus Area

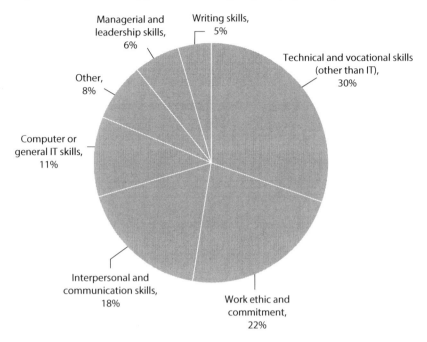

Managerial and leadership skills, 6%

Writing skills, 5%

Technical and vocational skills (other than IT), 30%

Other, 8%

Computer or general IT skills, 11%

Interpersonal and communication skills, 18%

Work ethic and commitment, 22%

Source: World Bank Philippine Enterprise Survey 2015; World Bank calculations.
Note: IT = information technology.

The next chapter examines the distribution of socioemotional skills in the Philippine labor force and estimates their value in the labor market. Wage data reveal that socioemotional skills command a significant and rising wage premium. The willingness of employers to pay higher wages to workers with socioemotional skills further underscores the scarcity and value of these skills in the Philippine labor market, as well as the economic gains the country could generate by narrowing the socioemotional skills gap.

Notes

1. In the World Bank Enterprise Surveys, construction firms are classified as service-sector firms.

2. This distinction is a simplification because a skills shortage is always a result of the demand for certain skills exceeding the supply, at a given wage level. The point is that, although the pool of skilled labor is much bigger in large than small cities, so is demand, which in both cases results in a skills shortage.

3. Variables that are not independently correlated with a reported skills gap include firm size, growth status, export orientation, and having a website. Under some specifications, firms older than five years appear more likely to face a skills shortage than younger firms.

4. Remittance income also tends to raise reservation wages.

5. Many firms fired workers for both poor performance and lack of technical skills. As a result, the percentage of firms that fired workers for either of the two factors (27 percent) is smaller than the sum of percentages of firms that fired workers for poor performance (25 percent) and for lack of technical skills (14 percent).

6. The results of the international comparisons should be treated with due caution because the characteristics of training programs might have differed among countries (for example, duration, intensity, content, and so on).

7. Other variables included in the regression equation were the size of the locality, the firm's age, its growth trajectory, and its export orientation.

References

Aedo, Cristian, Jesko Hentschel, Javier Luque, and Martín Moreno. 2013. "From Occupations to Embedded Skills: A Cross-Country Comparison." Policy Research Working Paper 6560, World Bank, Washington, DC.

Busso, Matías, Marina Bassi, Sergio Urzúa, and Jaimie Vargas. 2012. *Disconnected: Skills, Education, and Employment in Latin America*. Washington, DC: Inter-American Development Bank.

Cunningham, Wendy, and Paula Villaseñor. 2014. "Employer Voices, Employer Demands, and Implications for Public Skills Development Policy Connecting the Labor and Education Sectors." *World Bank Research Observer* 31 (1): 102–34.

di Gropello, Emanuela, Hong Tan, and Prateek Tandon. 2010. *Skills for the Labor Market in the Philippines*. Directions in Development Series. Washington, DC: World Bank.

World Bank. 2009. *World Bank Enterprise Survey 2009*.

CHAPTER 3

Socioemotional Skills in the Philippine Labor Force

Introduction

This chapter presents the main findings of the Skills Toward Employability and Productivity (STEP) survey, the first internationally comparable assessment of socioemotional skills among the Philippine labor force. The analysis examines the distribution of socioemotional, cognitive, and technical skills among different groups of workers and identifies individual characteristics that correlate with high levels of socioemotional skill. It evaluates the relationship between socioemotional skills and educational outcomes, and estimates their respective effect on employment and wage rates.

Measuring Different Types of Workforce Skills

The literature on workforce skills typically groups them into three general categories: cognitive skills, technical skills, and socioemotional skills (see table 3.1 for a breakdown of the three categories). *Cognitive skills* are the traditional focus of education. They include literacy, reading comprehension, numeracy, critical thinking, and applied reasoning, among others. *Technical skills* are task-specific competencies that often require a mix of education, training, and work experience. *Socioemotional skills* are fundamentally different from cognitive and technical skills; they relate to individual behavior, personality, attitude, and mindset.

In recent years, researchers have attempted to more precisely analyze the role of socioemotional skills in the labor market. Although conventional indicators of human capital, such as educational attainment and vocational training, are adequate metrics for assessing cognitive and technical skills, they do not fully capture socioemotional skills levels. One challenge countries are facing is how to measure skills. Such tools are crucial to help governments formulate skills development

Table 3.1 Definitions of Skills Used in This Study

Skills	Skill type	Specific skill	Definition
Cognitive skills	Academic knowledge and reasoning	Math proficiency	Ability to perform basic arithmetic operations, such as addition, subtraction, multiplication, division, and percentage
		Reading proficiency	Ability to understand, evaluate, use, and engage with written texts
Technical skills	Task-specific competencies	Unique to each role	Ability to effectively execute the functions of a given position, often by operating equipment or performing administrative processes
Socioemotional skills	Achieving goals	Conscientiousness	Tendency to be organized, responsible, and hardworking
		Openness to experience	Appreciation for novelty and comfort with change
		Grit	Perseverance in the pursuit of long-term goals
	Working with others	Agreeableness	Tendency to act in a cooperative, unselfish manner
		Extraversion	Sociability and willingness to engage with new people
	Managing emotions	Emotional stability	Predictability and consistency in emotional reactions; the absence of rapid mood changes
		Decision making	Confidence when exercising authority and committing to a course of action

policy and can continue to evolve alongside rapidly changing market demands. For example, the Organisation for Economic Co-operation and Development (OECD) has been implementing since 2000 the Programme for International Student Assessment (PISA), a triennial international survey that aims to assess the skills and knowledge of 15-year-old students on science, mathematics, reading, collaborative problem solving, and financial literacy. The OECD has also been implementing since 2011 an international survey to measure adult skills—the Programme for the International Assessment of Adult Competencies (PIAAC), covering literacy, numeracy and problem-solving skills. Unfortunately, the Philippines does not yet participate in these international assessment tools (covering more than 70 countries to date).

The STEP assessment is a global initiative by the World Bank that strives to measure workforce skills in developing countries and, for the first time, to generate a set of internationally comparable data on socioemotional skills.[1] The World Bank developed the STEP assessment to provide analysts and policy makers with quantifiable, granular information on socioemotional skills. The STEP has been conducted in three rounds covering 14 countries. The most recent round included the Philippines. Similar to the PIAAC, which also assesses similar adult population groups, the STEP survey assesses cognitive and technical competencies. However, unlike the PIAAC, STEP gathers self-reported information on personality and behavior. Socioemotional skills in STEP reflect the so-called big five personality traits—conscientiousness,

Box 3.1 Understanding the "Big Five" Personality Traits

The "big five" personality trait model has been widely used in sociology, psychology, and related fields for over 20 years. During that time, researchers have steadily refined the methodology for measuring openness to experience, conscientiousness, extraversion, agreeableness, and emotional stability. They have also drawn important conclusions about how these skills relate to one another and to the demands of different work environments.

Although each trait has desirable aspects, not all big five traits are appropriate for each professional role. For example, individuals with high scores for conscientiousness tend to be self-disciplined, circumspect, and focused on long-term planning. These are generally positive qualities, but they may not be consistent with success in a position that requires spontaneity or swift reactions to changing circumstances. Similarly, individuals with high scores for agreeableness tend to be considerate and generous, but for that reason they may be reluctant to make hard decisions that involve trade-offs between competing interests. Other traits, such as extraversion, are not inherently positive or negative but merely reflect a specific way of interacting with the world. Some traits, such as emotional stability, are far more valuable in certain contexts than in others. Individuals with high scores for emotional stability may be indispensable in high-pressure situations, but their ability to maintain composure may be less relevant in low-pressure environments. The "big five" construct does not measure the abstract quality of an individual's personality. Rather, it outlines the features of that personality—features that may be more or less valuable, or more or less relevant, depending on the situation.

openness to experience, agreeableness, extraversion, and emotional stability (box 3.1)—as well as two addition behavior traits, grit and decision making. These seven traits are expected to influence an individual's ability to achieve goals (conscientiousness, openness to experience, and grit), work with others (agreeableness and extraversion), and manage emotions (emotional stability and decision making). The survey records respondents' education level, employment experiences, and demographic characteristics; and it analyzes how they use various skills at work and outside of work.

A nationally representative STEP survey of urban households was conducted in the Philippines between August and December of 2015.[2] The survey sampled 3,000 Filipinos between the ages of 15 and 64 who resided in urban areas. Participants were randomly selected on the basis of the 2010 population census (table 3.2). The sample represents an urban population of about 31.7 million,[3] one-third of whom reside in the National Capital Region (NCR) and the other two-thirds in other urban areas scattered across 12 regions, 39 provinces, and 114 municipalities.[4] The STEP sample is not representative of the rural population because the rural economy demands a very different set of skills from the urban economy (box 3.2).

Developing Socioemotional Skills for the Philippines' Labor Market
http://dx.doi.org/10.1596/978-1-4648-1191-3

Table 3.2 The Distribution of the STEP Survey Sample, by Region

Region	Percent
NCR—National Capital Region (Metro Manila)	32.6
Region I—Ilocos Region	2.3
Region II—Cagayan Valley	1.9
Region III—Central Luzon	12.1
Region IV-A—Calabarzon	18.5
Region V—Bicol	4.3
Region VI—Western Visayas	4.1
Region IX—Zamboanga Peninsula	4.0
Region X—Northern Mindanao	6.0
Region XI—Davao Region	5.7
Region XII—SOCCSKSARGEN	7.1
Region XIII—Caraga	1.0
CAR—Cordillera Administrative Region	0.5
Total	100

Source: World Bank STEP Household Survey 2015.
Note: SOCCSKSARGEN = South Cotabato, Cotabato, Sultan Kudarat, and Sarangani and General Santos.
CAR = Cordillera Administrative Region.

Box 3.2 Comparability of STEP with Other National Household Surveys

Comparing the basic characteristics of the STEP survey samples with those of the Labor Force Survey administered by the Philippine Statistics Authority reveals that the two instruments yield comparable data. Both samples are based on the population census, both were conducted during 2015, and both focus on related aspects of education and employment.

Figure B3.2.1 Labor Market Status in Urban Areas, STEP vs LFS

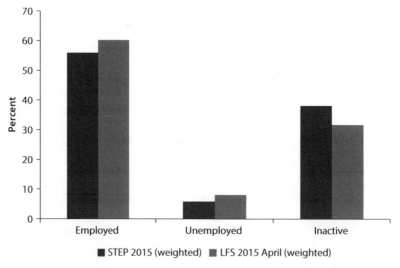

■ STEP 2015 (weighted)   ■ LFS 2015 April (weighted)

Source: World Bank STEP Household Survey 2015.
Note: LFS = Labor Force Survey; STEP = Skills Toward Employability and Productivity.

box continues next page

Box 3.2 Comparability of STEP with Other National Household Surveys *(continued)*

Figure B3.2.2 Educational Attainment among Working-Age Filipinos in Urban Areas, STEP vs LFS

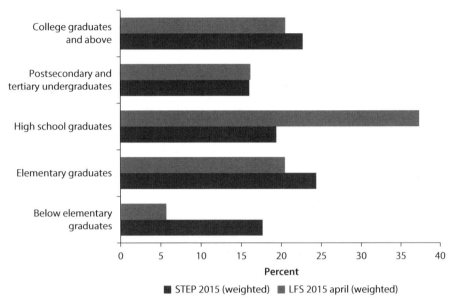

■ STEP 2015 (weighted) ■ LFS 2015 april (weighted)

Source: World Bank STEP Household Survey 2015.
Note: LFS = Labor Force Survey; STEP = Skills Toward Employability and Productivity.

Although the Labor Force Survey also captures information on the rural workforce, only its urban data are directly comparable to those produced by the STEP.

The basic characteristics of the two survey samples, such as gender composition, age distribution, and labor market status, are closely aligned (figure B3.2.1). However, they differ in terms of the average education level attained by respondents (figure B3.2.2). Although the share of the working-age population with some form of tertiary education is the same, the composition of respondents with a completed secondary education or an incomplete primary education differs significantly between the two surveys. The STEP sample includes a larger share of respondents with an incomplete primary education and a smaller share of respondents with a completed secondary education.

The Distribution of Skills in the Workforce

This section presents profiles of skills among the urban working-age populations of the Philippines. Observing the distribution of skills and traits allows us to establish skill profiles of these populations in the Philippines and to assess the extent to which skills differ by age, gender, and education level. These descriptive statistics are naturally influenced by simultaneous multiple factors that would influence the distribution and untangle their respective effects. However, they can be helpful to develop intuitive and basic interpretations on levels of skills stocks and how they are shared among the population.

Developing Socioemotional Skills for the Philippines' Labor Market
http://dx.doi.org/10.1596/978-1-4648-1191-3

Figure 3.1 Share of Respondents Who Passed the STEP Basic Literacy Test

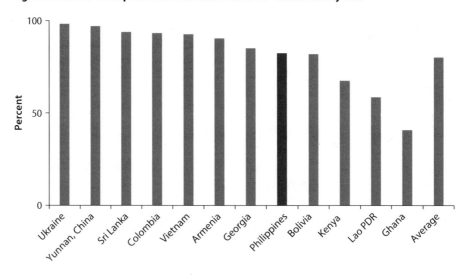

Source: World Bank STEP Household Surveys, various countries and years; World Bank calculations.
Note: STEP = Skills Toward Employability and Productivity.

Most working-age Filipinos passed the basic literacy test included in the STEP survey. The pass rate of 82 percent is similar to that of other developing countries (figure 3.1).[5] As would be expected, basic literacy is strongly correlated with educational level.

All measures of reading[6] and numeracy skills[7] are closely correlated with both education level and age. Older and more-educated respondents report reading more both at work and outside of work, with no significant gender difference (figure 3.2). Very few occupations require advanced mathematics, but more-educated respondents were marginally more likely to perform mathematical calculations at work and outside of work, with no significant difference by either age or gender (figure 3.3).

Although socioemotional skills are distributed almost identically between men and women, they vary substantially across age groups. The gender-neutral distribution of socioemotional skills (figure 3.4) has also been observed in other countries that administered the STEP survey. The disparity in socioemotional skills across age groups (figure 3.5) is similarly consistent with the international experience. Younger respondents tend to have lower scores across most indicators, and especially for grit, agreeableness, and decision making. Emotional stability is the only trait for which there was no significant correlation with age.

Education beyond the secondary level is correlated with strong socioemotional skills. There is a clear gap in the socioemotional skills possessed by respondents with incomplete secondary education or lower educational attainment levels, and those with completed secondary education or higher educational attainment levels. The distribution of each socioemotional skill was lower among less-educated respondents than their more-educated counterparts. The narrowest gaps were observed for emotional stability and conscientiousness (figure 3.6).

Figure 3.2 Length of Longest Documents Read at Work over the Past 12 Months

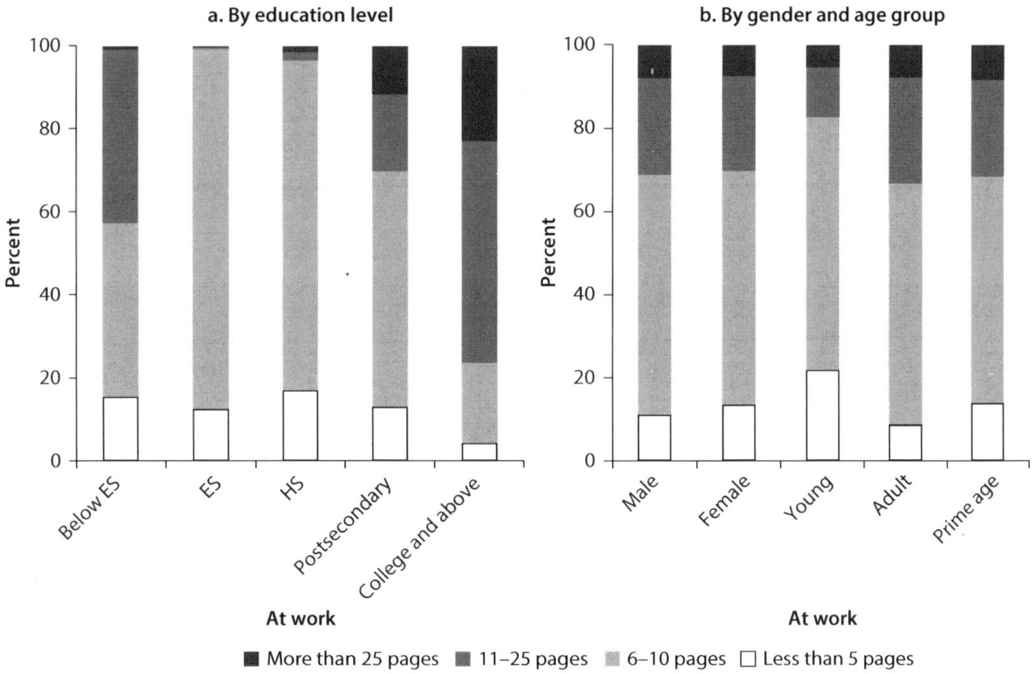

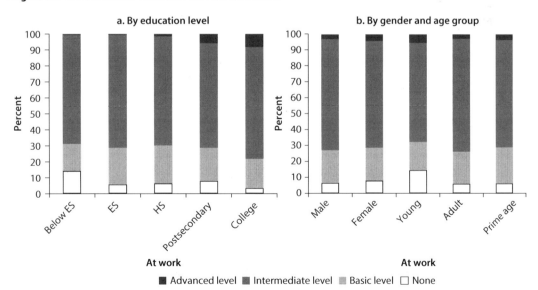

Source: World Bank STEP Household Survey 2015; World Bank calculations.
Note: ES = elementary school; HS = high school; Young = 15–24; Adult = 25–44; Prime age = 45–64.

Figure 3.3 Use of Math at Work over the Past 12 Months

Source: World Bank STEP Household Survey 2015; World Bank calculations.
Note: ES = elementary school; HS = high school; Young = 15–24; Adult = 25–44; Prime age = 45–64.

Developing Socioemotional Skills for the Philippines' Labor Market
http://dx.doi.org/10.1596/978-1-4648-1191-3

Figure 3.4 Distribution of Socioemotional Skills, by Gender

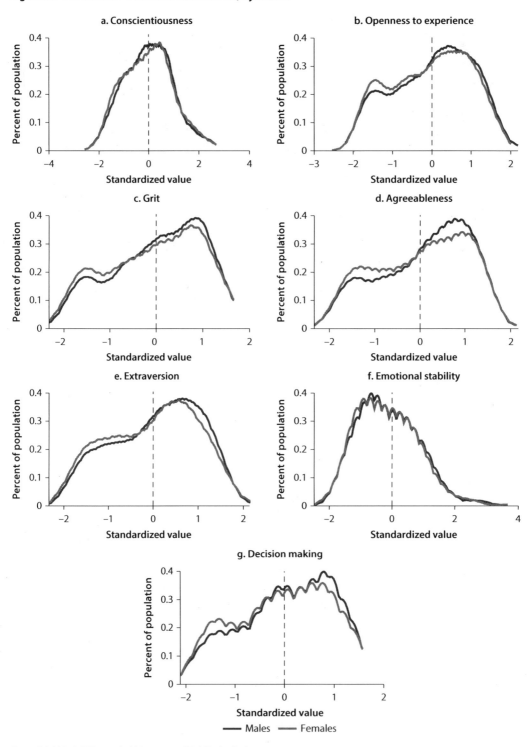

Source: World Bank STEP Household Survey 2015; World Bank calculations.

Figure 3.5 Distribution of Socioemotional Skills, by Age Group

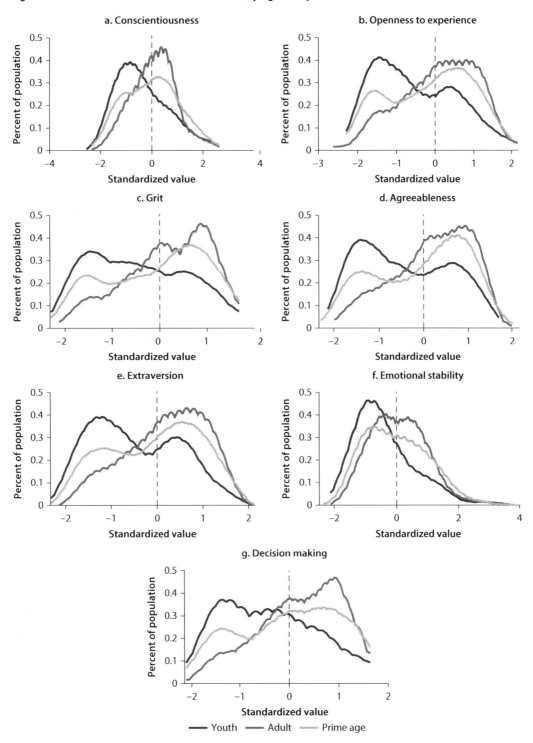

Source: World Bank STEP Household Survey 2015; World Bank calculations.
Note: Young = 15–24; Adult = 25–44; Prime age = 45–64.

Developing Socioemotional Skills for the Philippines' Labor Market
http://dx.doi.org/10.1596/978-1-4648-1191-3

Figure 3.6 Distribution of Socioemotional Skills, by Education Level

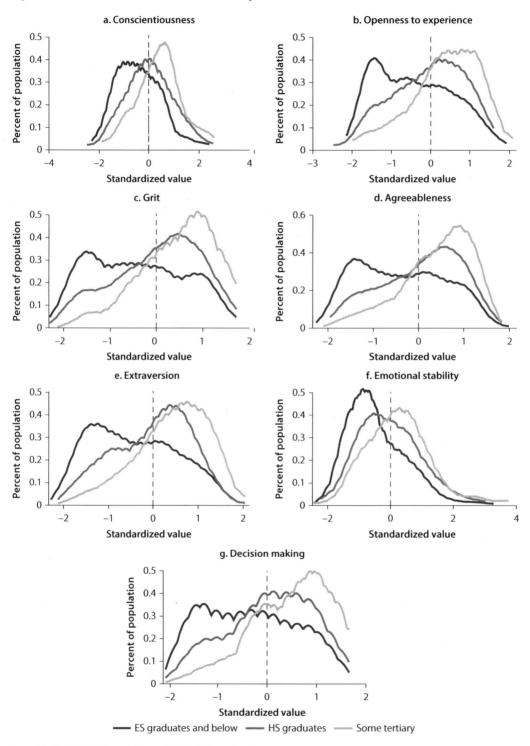

Source: World Bank STEP Household Survey 2015; World Bank calculations.
Note: ES = elementary school; HS = high school.

Employment status is also strongly correlated with greater socioemotional skills. Employed workers demonstrate higher socioemotional skills than unemployed workers across almost all indicators (figure 3.7). Employed workers are especially likely to have higher scores for grit, decision making, agreeableness, and extraversion. Emotional stability is the only indicator that does not vary with employment status.

Individual socioemotional skills closely correlate with one another. Respondents with high scores on any individual indicator of socioemotional skills are very likely to score highly on others, whereas respondents with low scores on any individual indicator are unlikely to score highly on others (table 3.3). Correlations between socioemotional skills were higher in the Philippines than in other countries for which STEP data are available.

In terms of technical skills, more-educated respondents are more likely to use nonroutine skills at work, whereas less-educated workers tend to focus on tasks that are routine and repetitive and that require physical labor. Educational attainment is positively correlated with nonroutine tasks such as personal interaction, presentation, supervision, thinking and learning, and autonomy (figure 3.8). Educational attainment is negatively correlated with physical labor and tasks that involve operating equipment, driving vehicles, and repairing machinery. Younger and older respondents tend to perform different job functions. Older workers are more likely

Figure 3.7 Distribution of Socioemotional Skills, by Employment Status

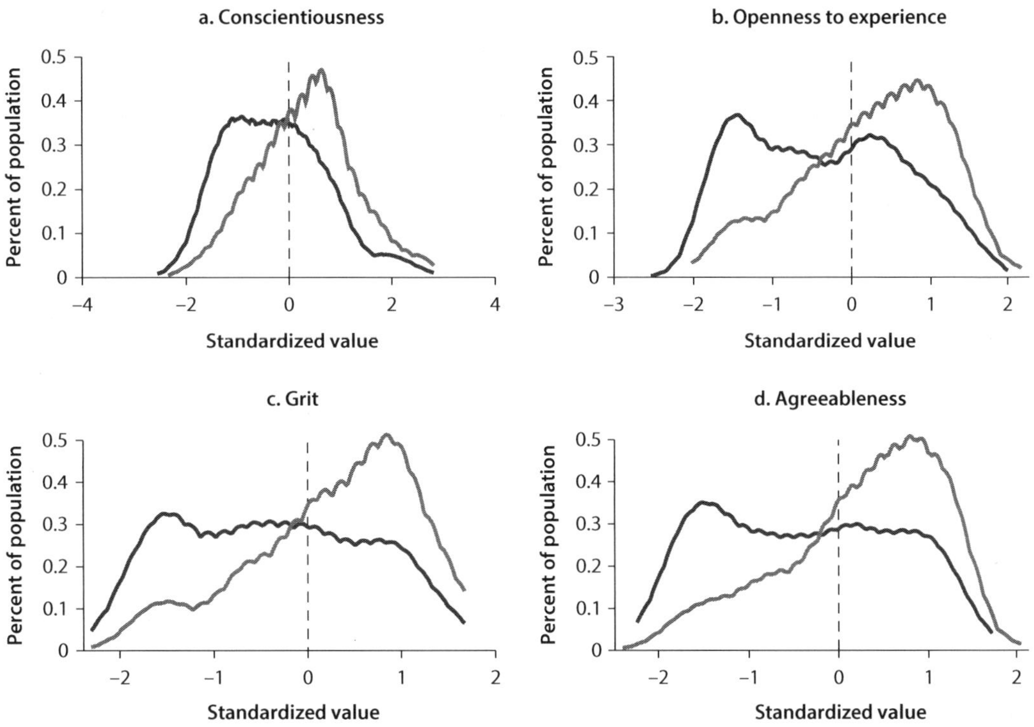

a. Conscientiousness

b. Openness to experience

c. Grit

d. Agreeableness

figure continues next page

Figure 3.7 Distribution of Socioemotional Skills, by Employment Status *(continued)*

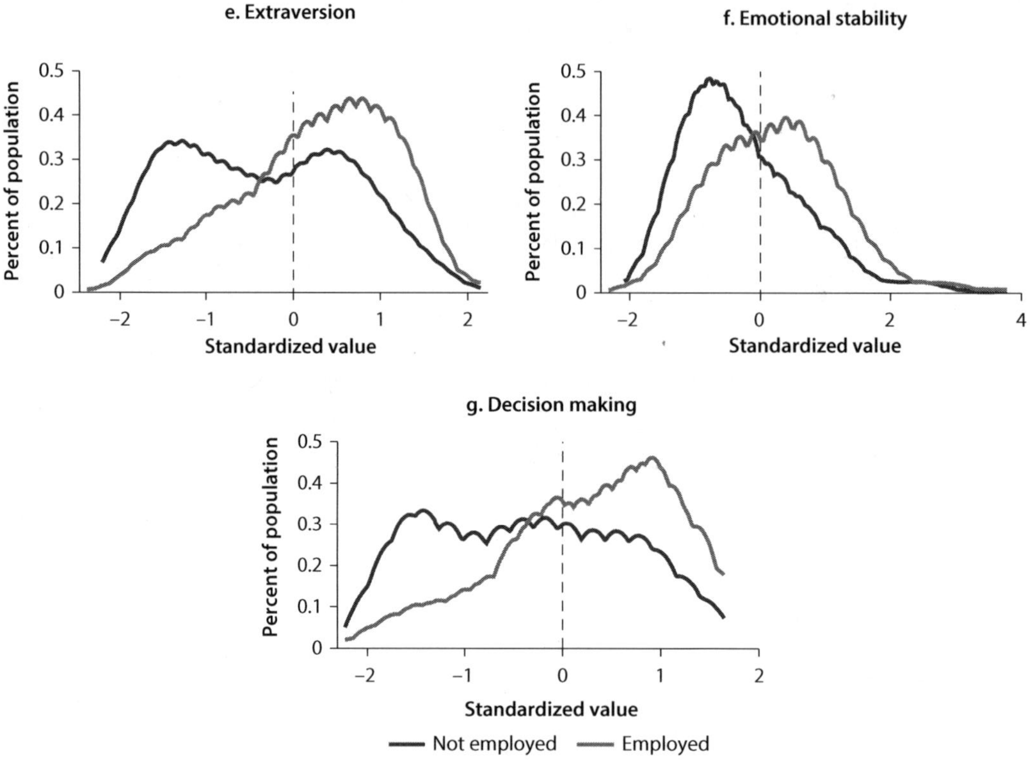

e. Extraversion

f. Emotional stability

g. Decision making

—— Not employed —— Employed

Source: World Bank STEP Household Survey 2015; World Bank calculations.

Table 3.3 Correlations between Socioemotional Skills

		(1)	(2)	(3)	(4)	(5)	(6)	(7)
(1)	Conscientiousness	1						
(2)	Openness to experience	0.781	1					
(3)	Grit	0.834	0.881	1				
(4)	Agreeableness	0.816	0.867	0.896	1			
(5)	Extraversion	0.785	0.878	0.884	0.879	1		
(6)	Emotional stability	0.699	0.631	0.660	0.650	0.639	1	
(7)	Decision making	0.806	0.859	0.897	0.879	0.864	0.646	1

Source: World Bank STEP Household Survey 2015; World Bank calculations.

to engage in tasks that require substantial thinking and autonomy, whereas younger workers are more likely to perform physical labor. Female workers are significantly more likely to engage in tasks that involve personal interaction.

Socioemotional skills are strongly correlated with certain technical skills. Respondents with lower socioemotional skill levels are more likely to possess physical skills, computer skills, or skills involving repetition. By contrast, respondents with higher levels of socioemotional skill tended to possess a wide range of technical skills, particularly skills related to communication, thinking, autonomy, and learning (figure 3.9).

Figure 3.8 Correlation Coefficients for Job Tasks and Years of Education, Gender, and Age

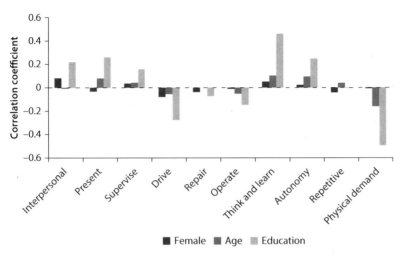

Source: World Bank STEP Household Survey 2015; World Bank calculations.

Figure 3.9 Correlations between Socioemotional Skills, Cognitive Skills, and Technical Skills

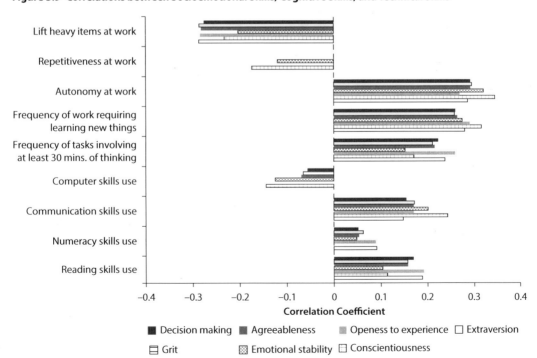

Source: World Bank STEP Household Survey 2015; World Bank calculations.
Note: Only correlation coefficients significant at the 95 percent level are shown.

In terms of subjective perceptions, one in four respondents reported being concerned about his or her perceived lack of skills. This rate is high by international standards, and concern about lack of skills is particularly acute among less-educated workers. More than 30 percent of respondents who did not complete primary school cite their lack of skills as a significant constraint on their employment, wage, promotion, and entrepreneurship prospects. Conversely, more-educated workers typically do not view lack of skills as an obstacle to their professional success (figure 3.10).

Less-educated workers tend to doubt the value of their education in the workplace, but the same is true for a substantial share of workers with tertiary education. At least 70 percent of respondents with completed secondary education or less believe that what they studied in school is not relevant, or is only marginally relevant, to the demands of their workplace. It is surprising that more than half of respondents who had completed postsecondary technical and vocational education and training, as well as a third of respondents with completed tertiary education, also report that their qualifications are of dubious usefulness in the workplace. Nevertheless, respondents with completed tertiary education are more likely than any other group to describe their education as relevant to their work (figure 3.11).

Although a large share of workers report concerns regarding the relevance of their job skills and a large share of firms provide training to their workers, education level is directly correlated with training and inversely correlated with reported concerns. About 20 percent of workers with completed tertiary education report having been trained by their employer; the same is true for only 3 percent of workers with completed secondary education or less. Although less-educated workers are systematically more likely to regard lack of job skills as an obstacle to professional success, they are also systematically less likely to receive employer training.

Figure 3.10 Share of Respondents Citing Lack of Literacy or Computer Skills as an Obstacle to Employment or Promotion

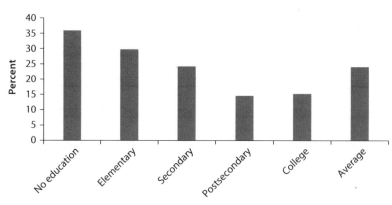

Source: World Bank STEP Household Survey 2015; World Bank calculations.

Figure 3.11 Share of Workers Reporting That Their Formal Education Is Useful in the Workplace

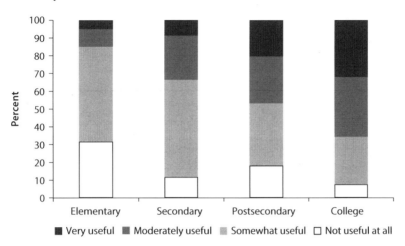

Source: World Bank STEP Household Survey 2015; World Bank calculations.

Labor-Market Returns to Socioemotional Skills

The STEP data shed light on the complex relation between socioemotional skills and labor market outcomes in the Philippines. Before examining that relation, a few key features of the labor market should be emphasized. First, more than half of working-age women and young people are either unemployed or not participating in the labor force. Second, average wages correlate closely with age and education level (table 3.4). Workers with completed secondary education earn twice as much as workers with completed primary education or less, and workers with tertiary education earn even more. Older workers tend to have been employed at their most recent job for significantly longer than younger workers, and seniority likely contributes to their higher wage rates.

Overall, urban workers with higher levels of socioemotional skills tend to receive higher wages.[8] All socioemotional skills except emotional stability have a significant effect on wages (figure 3.12). Although one additional year of education is associated with a 3 percent wage increase (holding socioemotional skills, cognitive skills, and personal characteristics constant), an increase of one standard deviation in socioemotional skill level is associated with 5.6–9.0 percent wage increase, or an additional US$2 per day over the average wage.[9] See box 3.3 for a discussion of the calculation of returns to skills.

Among socioemotional skills, extraversion and openness to new experiences have an especially strong correlation with earning. About 26 percent of respondents scored one standard deviation below the average for indicators of extraversion and openness to experience, whereas 36 percent of respondents scored at the mean. The magnitude of the wage difference between these two groups was equal to the wage differential between respondents with completed primary and

Table 3.4 Labor-Market Outcomes by Worker Characteristics

Characteristic	Probability of being employed (%)	Wage (pesos/hour)	Time employed at most recent job (months)
All	56	82	83
Gender			
Male	67	76	101
Female	46	90	90
Age (years)			
Youth (15–24)	43	65	40
Adults (25–44)	58	83	92
Prime age (45–64)	55	79	85
Education			
Completed primary or less	56	44	99
Completed secondary	54	82	117
Incomplete tertiary	61	86	85
Completed tertiary	57	146	84

Source: World Bank STEP Household Survey 2015; World Bank calculations.

Figure 3.12 Wage Differences Associated with Socioemotional Skills, Cognitive Skills, and Education

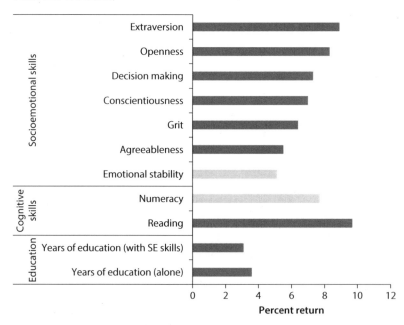

Source: World Bank STEP Household Survey 2015; World Bank calculations.
Note: Solid bars indicate statistical significance at the 95 percent confidence level; faded bars indicate no statistical significance. Conditional correlations are based on ordinary least squares regressions controlling for gender, age, age squared, occupation, maternal education, and region. Personality traits are standardized. SE = socioemotional.

Box 3.3 Methodological Considerations in Estimating Associations between Skills, Labor Market Outcomes, and Educational Trajectories

This analysis uses Mincerean wage equations to estimate the returns to skills in the labor market. These equations estimate levels of association between the natural log of labor earnings and characteristics such as years of education and socioemotional skills, represented by the big five personality traits plus grit and decision making. Measures of reading and mathematical proficiency are used as proxies for cognitive skills. The equations also control for individual characteristics such as age, gender, maternal education level, primary occupation, and region. The effect of socioemotional skills and cognitive skills on educational attainment, employment, and wages (conditional on the control variables) is determined by a standard microeconometric Mincerean model:

$$Y_i = \alpha + \beta_1 A_i + \beta_2 X_i + \varepsilon_i \tag{B3.3.1}$$

where Y_i is a labor-market or educational outcome (for example, wages, employment probability, job type, or years of education), A_i represents all skills that affect the outcome (for example, reading proficiency, numeracy, conscientiousness, decision making), and X_i represents all other factors that affect Y_i (for example, gender, age, region).

Indeed, it is now well known that educational attainment is an inadequate proxy for cognitive or socioemotional skill because (i) many cognitive and socioemotional skills are acquired outside the classroom and (ii) the skills that are acquired in the classroom vary widely across schools and countries (Hanushek and Woessman 2008). However, the STEP data include test scores, T_i, that can capture dimensions of basic cognitive, socioemotional, and even technical skills. Assuming T_i measures all skills captured in equation B3.3.1, the equation can be rewritten as follows:

$$Y_i = \alpha + \beta_1 T_i + \beta_2 X_i + v_i \tag{B3.3.2}$$

If the sets of T_i perfectly measure vector A_i, equation B3.3.2 can be estimated using the ordinary least squares (OLS) method (for wages) or a logit function (for probability of employment and other discrete outcomes) without any skill bias, and β_1 will indicate the return to each skill captured by vector T_i. However, a growing literature shows that measured skills represented by T_i capture A_i with error, so dependence between T_i and the error term v_i could be possible (that is, $Cov\,(T_i, v_i) \neq 0$). In that case, measurement errors and omitted variables could produce biased estimates of β_1. Therefore, this method cannot conclusively identify a causal relationship between measured skills and labor market outcomes. Because of the cross-sectional nature of the data, both the measured skills and the outcomes are observed simultaneously. In other words, employment status or job type could also influence individual cognitive and socioemotional skills. Previous studies have employed alternative methodologies to overcome this challenge, yielding similar results to those generated by simple OLS estimations (Cunningham, Acosta, and Muller 2016). Moreover, the literature indicates that most skills are well established by early adulthood (see chapter 4), further diminishing the possibility of reverse causation. Nevertheless, the results should be interpreted with caution.

---

completed secondary education. In other words, the reduction in wages associated with scoring one standard deviation below the mean for these socioemotional skills is comparable to the reduction in wages associated with not having a high school diploma.

Female workers drive the correlation between socioemotional skills and wages. Among male workers, most socioemotional skills are not significantly correlated with wages. Among female workers, however, the wage premium associated with a one-standard-deviation increase in socioemotional skill exceeds the premium associated with an additional year of education (figure 3.13). Female workers with high scores for openness to new experiences, extraversion, decision making, grit, and conscientiousness receive especially high wage premiums. Among male workers, only extraversion is associated with higher wages. The returns to education and cognitive skills are marginally higher for male workers than for female workers.

Socioemotional skills are especially valuable to younger workers. The effect of socioemotional skills on wages is especially strong for workers younger than

Figure 3.13 Wage Differences Associated with Socioemotional Skills, Cognitive Skills, and Education, by Gender

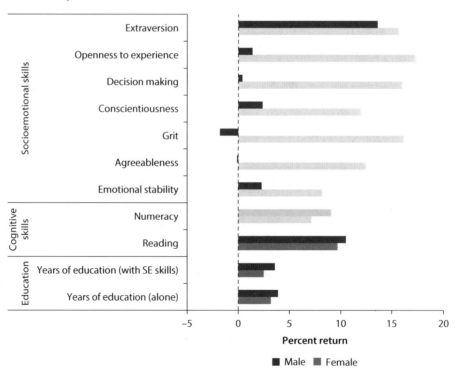

Source: World Bank STEP Household Survey 2015; World Bank calculations.
Note: Solid bars indicate statistical significance at the 95 percent confidence level; faded bars indicate no statistical significance. Conditional correlations are based on ordinary least squares regressions controlling for, age, age squared, occupation, maternal education, and region. Personality traits are standardized. SE = socioemotional.

Figure 3.14 Wage Differences Associated with Socioemotional Skills, Cognitive Skills, and Education, by Age

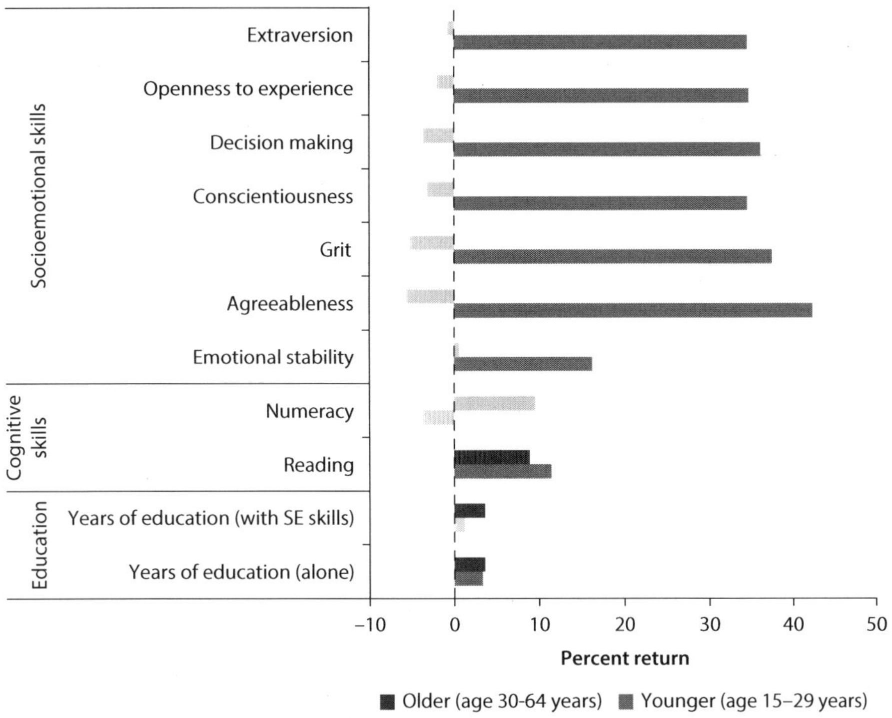

Source: World Bank STEP Household Survey 2015; World Bank calculations.
Note: Solid bars indicate statistical significance at the 95 percent confidence level; faded bars indicate no statistical significance. Conditional correlations are based on ordinary least squares regressions controlling for gender, occupation, maternal education, and region. Personality traits are standardized. SE = socioemotional.

30 years old (figure 3.14). Among younger workers, a high level of agreeableness is associated with a 40 percent increase in wages. Among older workers, however, socioemotional skills are more weakly correlated with wages. Although younger workers tend to have lower scores for most socioemotional skills, each incremental improvement yields a substantial wage premium. By contrast, the returns associated with more years of education and more use of numeracy skills are larger for older workers.

The wage premium associated with socioemotional skills is highest among less-educated workers. Extraversion, conscientiousness, openness to new experiences, agreeableness, and decision making correlate with substantial increases in wages for less-educated workers, but not for their more-educated counterparts (figure 3.15). Meanwhile, use of numeracy skills is associated with a wage premium only among highly educated workers. This implies that socioemotional skills tend to substitute for, rather than complement, more traditional cognitive and technical skills, and that they can offer a route to higher earnings for workers with limited formal education.

Developing Socioemotional Skills for the Philippines' Labor Market
http://dx.doi.org/10.1596/978-1-4648-1191-3

Figure 3.15 Wage Differences Associated with Socioemotional Skills, Cognitive Skills, and Education, by Education Level

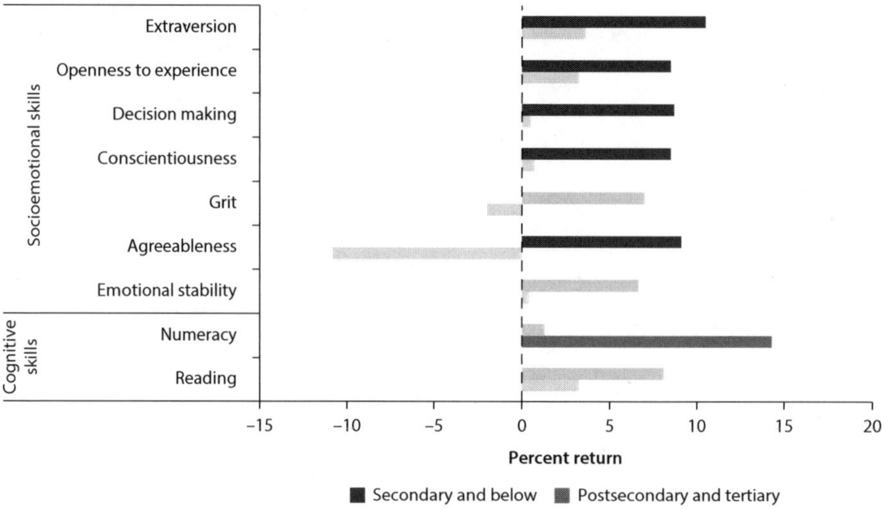

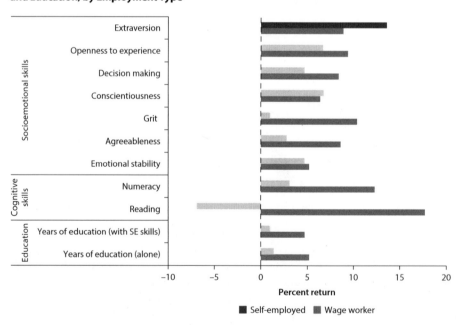

Source: World Bank STEP Household Survey 2015; World Bank calculations.
Note: Solid bars indicate statistical significance at the 95 percent confidence level, faded bars indicate no statistical significance. Conditional correlations are based on ordinary least squares regressions controlling for gender, age, age squared, occupation, maternal education, and region. Personality traits are standardized.

Figure 3.16 Wage Differences Associated with Socioemotional Skills, Cognitive Skills, and Education, by Employment Type

Source: World Bank STEP Household Survey 2015; World Bank calculations.
Note: Solid bars indicate statistical significance at the 95 percent confidence level; faded bars indicate no statistical significance. Conditional correlations based on ordinary least squares regressions controlling for gender, age, age-squared, occupation, maternal education, and region. Personality traits are standardized. SE = socioemotional.

Among workers employed by a firm, a wide range of socioemotional and cognitive skills is associated with higher wages (figure 3.16). Among self-employed workers, however, only extraversion is associated with increased income; correlations with all other socioemotional skills and cognitive skills are insignificant.

Socioemotional skills are associated with higher wages only in the service sector. Socioemotional skills are not significantly correlated with wages among workers in the agricultural and manufacturing sectors, but in the service sector high levels of socioemotional skills are associated with wage premiums of about 10 percent (figure 3.17). More years of education are associated with higher wages in all sectors. The wage premium for socioemotional skills in the service sector may encourage workers with higher levels of socioemotional skill to seek employment in that sector.

Tasks requiring specific technical skills are also associated with higher wages. Workers who regularly employ numeracy skills, use computers, and frequently learn new things at work tend to receive higher wages (figure 3.18). By contrast, performing repetitive tasks is associated with lower wages, while

Figure 3.17 Wage Differences Associated with Socioemotional Skills, Cognitive Skills, and Education, by Economic Sector

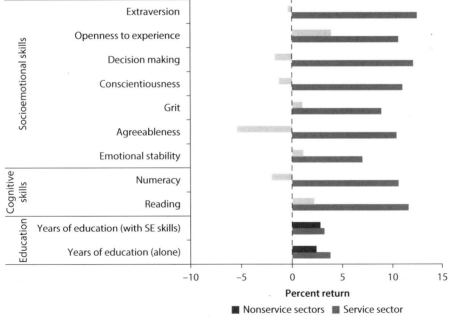

Source: World Bank STEP Household Survey 2015; World Bank calculations.
Note: Solid bars indicate statistical significance at the 95 percent confidence level; faded bars indicate no statistical significance. Conditional correlations are based on ordinary least squares regressions controlling for gender, age, age squared, occupation, maternal education, and region. Personality traits are standardized. SE = socioemotional.

Figure 3.18 Wage Differences Associated with Tasks Involving Technical Skills

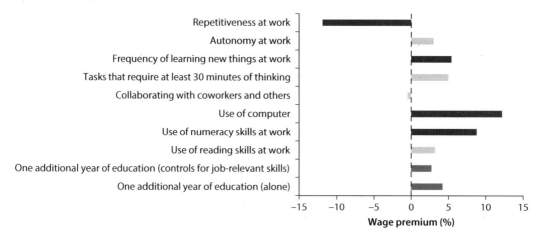

Source: World Bank STEP Household Survey 2015; World Bank calculations.
Note: Solid bars indicate statistical significance at the 95 percent confidence level; faded bars indicate no statistical significance. Conditional correlations are based on ordinary least squares regressions controlling for gender, age, age squared, occupation, maternal education, and region.

tasks involving substantial reading, thinking, autonomy, and collaboration are not significantly correlated with wages.

Socioemotional Skills and Employment Probability

The STEP survey found that years of education are not correlated with the probability of being employed, but that workers with strong socioemotional skills are more likely to be employed. An increase of one standard deviation in socioemotional skill levels is associated with a 15-percentage-point increase in employment probability. In other words, an increase of one standard deviation in socioemotional skills raises the average probability of employment from 0.56 to 0.7 (figure 3.19). Increased numeracy is also associated with a greater probability of employment, whereas propensity to read is inversely correlated with employment probability.[10]

Across subgroups, differences in employment probability are smaller than the wage premiums associated with socioemotional skills. Like wage premiums, employment probability is most strongly correlated with socioemotional skills among female workers (figure 3.20). However, unlike wage premiums, socioemotional skills are more strongly correlated with employment among older workers and more-educated workers (figure 3.21). Education is not significantly correlated to employment probability, but propensity to use numeracy skills is positively correlated with employment probability, especially among less-educated workers.

Figure 3.19 Correlations between Socioemotional Skills, Cognitive Skills, and Education, and Changes in Employment Probability

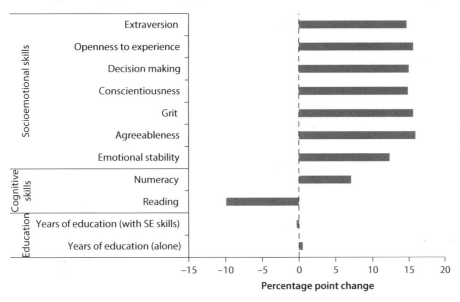

Source: World Bank STEP Household Survey 2015; World Bank calculations.
Note: Solid bars indicate statistical significance at the 95 percent confidence level; faded bars indicate no statistical significance. Marginal effects on employment probability are based on a probit model that controls for standardized personality traits, gender, age, age squared, maternal education, and region. SE = socioemotional.

Figure 3.20 Socioemotional Skills, Cognitive Skills, Education, and Employment Probability, by Gender

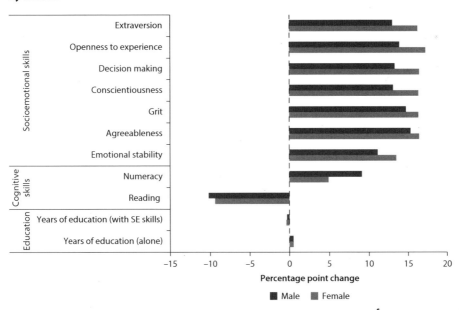

Source: World Bank STEP Household Survey 2015; World Bank calculations.
Note: Solid bars indicate statistical significance at the 95 percent confidence level; faded bars indicate no statistical significance. Marginal effects on employment probability are based on a probit model that controls for standardized personality traits, gender, age, age squared, maternal education, and region. SE = socioemotional.

Figure 3.21 Socioemotional Skills, Cognitive Skills, Education, and Employment Probability, by Education Level

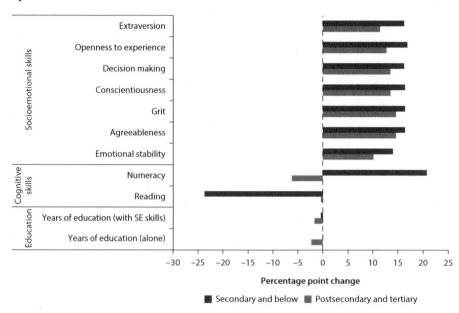

Source: World Bank STEP Household Survey 2015; World Bank calculations.
Note: Solid bars indicate statistical significance at the 95 percent confidence level; faded bars indicate no statistical significance. Marginal effects on employment probability are based on a probit model that controls for standardized personality traits, gender, age, age squared, maternal education, and region. SE = socioemotional.

Socioemotional Skills and Educational Attainment

Educational attainment influences skills development, and skills development influences educational attainment. Although cognitive and socioemotional skills can be taught in school, those same skills can also affect a range of educational outcomes (Duncan et al. 2007). The development of basic cognitive skills at a young age can affect a student's success throughout his or her academic career. Socioemotional skills can also influence educational attainment. A major study of longitudinal data from the United States found that socioemotional skills explain 12 percent of the variations in educational attainment between individuals, whereas cognitive skills explain another 16 percent (Cunha, Heckman, and Schennach 2010).

In the Philippines, workers with higher socioemotional skill levels are more likely to have completed secondary education. Controlling for the same characteristics as in the analysis above, conscientiousness is the skill most strongly correlated with completing secondary education (figure 3.22). Decision making and grit are also associated with completing secondary education. Among cognitive skills, propensity to read is closely linked to secondary completion, but numeracy is not. These findings suggest that socioemotional skills play a role comparable to that of cognitive skills in determining educational outcomes.[11]

Socioemotional skills are also closely correlated with pursuing—though not necessarily completing—tertiary education. All socioemotional skills are

Box 3.4 Workforce Skills and Labor Market Outcomes in Other Developing Countries

Socioemotional skills appear to influence labor-market outcomes in the Philippines to a much greater extent than in other developing countries. In the Philippines, a one-standard-deviation change in socioemotional skills is associated with a 12-percentage-point increase in employment probability. In Georgia and Vietnam, socioemotional skills are also associated with greater employment probability, but the magnitude of the increase is much smaller (figure B3.4.1). In Colombia, conscientiousness is the only socioemotional skill associated with a greater probability of employment. Whereas years of education are not correlated with employment probability in the Philippines, greater education attainment is closely correlated with employment in Georgia and Vietnam. Georgia and the Philippines both evince a positive relationship between numeracy and employment,

Figure B3.4.1 Socioemotional Skills, Cognitive Skills, Education, and Employment Probability, Philippines and Select Comparators

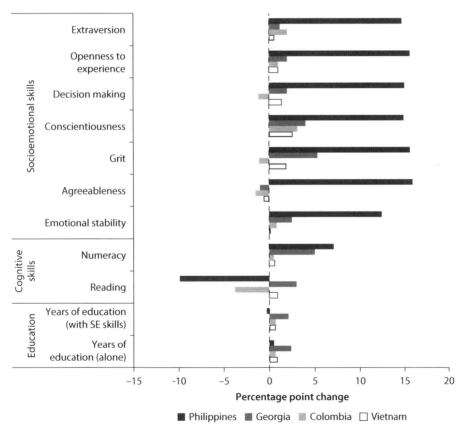

Source: World Bank STEP Household Surveys, various countries, most recent years; World Bank calculations.
Note: Marginal effects on employment probability are based on a probit model that controls for standardized personality traits, gender, age, age squared, maternal education, and region. SE = socioemotional.

box continues next page

Box 3.4 Workforce Skills and Labor Market Outcomes in Other Developing Countries *(continued)*

whereas the Philippines and Vietnam display the same negative correlation between employment probability and propensity to read.

The wage premium associated with socioemotional skills is both significantly higher and more consistent across skills in the Philippines than it is in comparable countries. Conscientiousness and emotional stability are linked to higher wages in Vietnam, conscientiousness and decision making are associated with higher wages in Georgia, and openness to experience correlates with higher wages in Colombia (figure B3.4.2). However, in each comparator country, the wage premium associated with socioemotional skills is much smaller than in the Philippines. Conversely, more years of education are associated with a smaller wage increase in the Philippines than in any of its comparators. The wage premium associated with a propensity to read is higher in the Philippines, whereas the premium associated with numeracy is lower.

Figure B3.4.2 Socioemotional Skills, Cognitive Skills, Education, and Wages, Philippines and Select Comparators

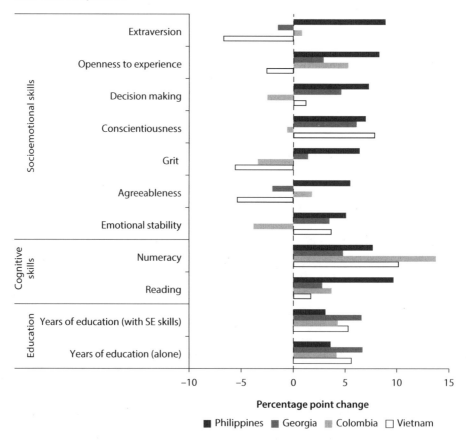

Source: World Bank STEP Household Surveys, various countries, most recent years; World Bank calculations.
Note: Conditional correlations are based on ordinary least square regressions controlling for gender, age, age squared, occupation, maternal education, and region. Personality traits are standardized. SE = socioemotional.

Figure 3.22 The Marginal Impact of Socioemotional Skills on Secondary School Completion

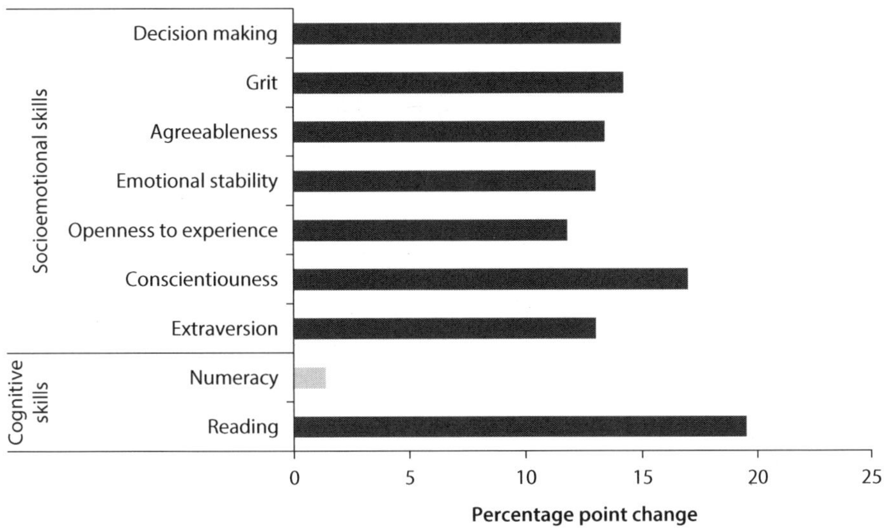

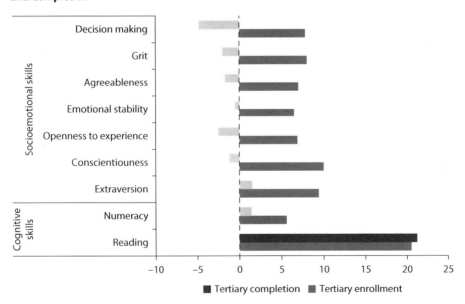

Source: World Bank STEP Household Survey 2015; World Bank calculations.
Note: Solid bars indicate statistical significance at the 95 percent confidence level; faded bars indicate no statistical significance. Marginal effects on school completion probability are based on a probit model that controls for standardized personality traits, gender, age, age squared, maternal education, and region.

Figure 3.23 The Marginal Impact of Socioemotional Skills on Tertiary Enrollment and Completion

Source: World Bank STEP Household Survey 2015; World Bank calculations.
Note: Solid bars indicate statistical significance at the 95 percent confidence level; faded bars indicate no statistical significance. Marginal effects on enrollment and school completions probability are based on a probit model that controls for standardized personality traits, gender, age, age squared, maternal education, and region. The results presented are for a subsample of respondents with completed secondary education.

Developing Socioemotional Skills for the Philippines' Labor Market
http://dx.doi.org/10.1596/978-1-4648-1191-3

associated with an increased probability of enrolling in tertiary education, but no socioemotional skill is significantly correlated with tertiary completion. Among cognitive skills, numeracy is associated with an increased probability of tertiary enrollment, but is not correlated with tertiary completion, whereas propensity to read is associated with a dramatic increase in the probability of both enrolling in and completing tertiary education (figure 3.23).

The evidence presented in this chapter reveals the importance of socioemotional skills to labor market outcomes and educational attainment. The STEP data show that the Philippine labor market rewards workers who possess strong socioemotional skills with higher wages and a greater possibility of employment. Moreover, socioemotional skills are also closely correlated with higher rates of secondary school completion and tertiary enrollment. The final chapter examines the extent to which the Philippine education sector fosters the development of socioemotional skills, situates its performance in the international context, and provides recommendations for policy interventions and structural reforms.

Notes

1. For more information on the World Bank STEP assessment, visit http://microdata .worldbank.org/index.php/catalog/step/about.

2. Actual interviews in the STEP survey were conducted in two stages by local enumerators using the standardized questionnaire. In the first stage, a comprehensive household roster was created that captured all family members and their basic individual information and from which one respondent, between the ages of 15 and 64 years, was randomly drawn. In this stage, the information related to asset holdings was also captured. In the second stage, the main survey modules gathering individual information on education, training, employment history, personality and behavior, physical well-being, use of skills at work and home, and family background were administered to the selected respondent. After the interview, the direct assessments were administered. Training, knowledge-testing, and field-pilot training were conducted with enumerators before the field work. The postsurvey data check and random spot-checks were also administered to validate the accuracy of the collected information. The refusal rate was maintained at 5.2 percent, which was low relative to STEP surveys in other countries.

3. The urban population is defined as residents of urban *barangays*. A barangay is the country's smallest political unit, and the Philippine Statistics Authority classifies barangays as either urban or rural. Urban barangays have a population of 5,000 or more, at least one firm with a minimum of 100 employees, five or more firms with 10 to 99 employees, and five or more facilities within a two-kilometer radius of the barangay hall.

4. A full description of the sampling methodology is available upon request.

5. Besides basic literacy, the STEP survey attempts to gauge reading comprehension. However, the data produced by this survey section have been found to lack statistical reliability in international comparisons. This report therefore excludes that part of the assessment.

6. STEP respondents report their use of reading skills in terms of the number of pages of the longest document they read during the past 12 months. These documents

include e-mails, forms, bills and financial statements, newspapers, magazines, operational manuals, books, and other forms of text.

7. STEP respondents report their use of numeracy skills in terms of the frequency with which they measure and estimate sizes, weights, and distances; calculate prices or costs; perform multiplication or division; calculate fractions, decimals, or percentages; and use algebra, geometry, trigonometry, or other forms of advanced math.

8. To minimize multicollinearity concerns arising from the strong correlation between individual socioemotional skills (table 3.3), each skill measure is entered individually in the regressions. The results of the regression analysis are presented in appendix A. Regression results for personal characteristics are available upon request.

9. Tables for subgroups are available upon request.

10. See appendix A for the main regression tables. Tables for subgroups are available upon request.

11. See appendix A for the main regression tables. Tables for subgroups are available upon request.

References

Cunha, Flavio, James Heckman, and Susanne Schennach. 2010. "Estimating the Technology of Cognitive and Noncognitive Skill Formation." *Econometrica* 78 (3): 883–931.

Cunningham, Wendy, Pablo Acosta, and Noël Muller. 2016. *Minds and Behaviors at Work: Boosting Socioemotional Skills for Latin America's Workforce*. Directions in Development Series. Washington, DC: World Bank.

Duncan, Greg J., Chantelle J. Dowsett, Amy Claessens, Katherine Magnuson, Aletha C. Huston, Pamela Kato Klebanov, Linda Pagani, Leon Feinstein, Mimi Engel, Jeanne Brooks-Gunn, Holly Sexton, and Kathryn Duckworth. 2007. "School Readiness and Later Achievement." *Developmental Psychology* 43 (6): 1428–46.

Hanushek, Eric A., and Ludger Woessman. 2008. "The Role of Cognitive Skills in Economic Development." *Journal of Economic Literature* 46: 607–68.

CHAPTER 4

Promoting the Development of Socioemotional Skills in the Philippines

Introduction

The analysis presented in previous chapters has highlighted the critical importance of socioemotional skills to both employment outcomes and educational attainment, yet the Philippine education sector has only recently begun to actively foster their development of socioemotional skills. The Philippines lags other developing countries in terms of mainstreaming socioemotional skills development into public policy. The international experience indicates that primary school is an optimal period for developing these critical skills, but the Philippine educational system continues to focus almost exclusively on teaching traditional cognitive skills. Integrating socioemotional skills into the education paradigm will be a complex process, but successfully enhancing the socioemotional skills of the Philippine labor force could have a highly positive effect on economic growth, competitiveness, poverty reduction, and shared prosperity.

Critical Stages to Foster the Development of Socioemotional Skills

Recent studies have found that the most critical period for developing socioemotional skills is between the ages of 6 and 11 (Heckman, Stixrud, and Urzúa 2006; Guerra, Modecki, and Cunningham 2014; Cunningham, Acosta, and Muller 2016). Building socioemotional skills is a continuous and progressive process, which begins shortly after birth and continues through adulthood. However, interventions during middle childhood appear to have the greatest effect because children between 6 and 11 possess both the neurobiological capacity and the psychosocial maturity to effectively practice and learn socioemotional skills. Interventions in middle childhood can pave the way for the further development of these skills during adolescence: socioemotional development interventions should continue through secondary school, and they should not be limited to at-risk youth. Schools are the ideal setting in which to teach these skills because the school environment has greatest influence of any public institution over children and teenagers (see box 4.1 for further discussion of the best ages for teaching various skills).

A number of programs foster socioemotional skills before, during, or after school to achieve diverse objectives such as child development or labor

---

Box 4.1 The PRACTICE Model

Guerra, Modecki, and Cunningham (2014) identify the optimal ages for developing socioemotional skills by analyzing data from employer surveys. The study groups socioemotional skills into eight categories of values and behaviors that are assets in the labor market. This classification is summarized by the acronym PRACTICE: Problem-solving, Resilience, Achievement motivation, self-Control, Teamwork, Initiative, Confidence, and Ethics.

Each of the skills that contribute to PRACTICE values and behaviors can be taught most effectively at a specific age (table B4.1.1). For example, problem solving is best developed during middle childhood (ages 6–11 years) and adolescence (ages 12–18 years). Foundational problem-solving skills can be developed in early childhood (ages 0–5 years) and reinforced in early adulthood (ages 19–29 years).

Table B4.1.1 Optimal Stages of Development for PRACTICE Skills

		Optimal age for development (years)			
Socioemotional skills	Values and behaviors	0–5	6–11	2–18	9–29
Conscientiousness	Problem solving	F	O	O	R
Conscientiousness/grit Resilience	Resilience	O	O	R	
Conscientiousness Openness to experience	Achieve motivation		O	R	
Conscientiousness	Control	O	O	O	R
Extraversion Agreeableness	Teamwork	O	O	R	
Conscientiousness Openness to experience	Initiative	O	O	O	O
Resilience	Confidence	F	O	O	R
Conscientiousness	Ethics	F	O	O	

Note: F = foundational stage; O = optimal stage; R = reinforcement stage.

Middle childhood is the optimal period for developing every PRACTICE skill. Adolescence is the second-most critical formative period, and it allows for the elaboration of skills developed in middle childhood. A concerted and holistic approach to socioemotional development should involve different interventions in early childhood, middle childhood, adolescence, and adulthood. However, because of the pivotal nature of the middle childhood period, efforts to foster the development of socioemotional skills should focus on primary school.

---

market–related outcomes. Such programs offer a range of different services and target diverse population groups. Importantly, many interventions claim to include "socioemotional skills," "life skills," or "soft skills"; but few explicitly state exactly which skills they intend to improve. However, academic evaluations rarely measure socioemotional skills development, and substantial additional research will be necessary to accurately evaluate the impact of socioemotional skills–development programs (Sanchez Puerta, Valerio, and Bernal 2016).

Such interventions have been implemented, and evaluated, across the world. Various programs targeted to different age levels, engaging appropriate actors, and using age-appropriate concepts and methodologies show that socioemotional skills development can occur in a structured environment outside the home. This suggests that the development of such skills, although taught in the home—particularly for certain ages—can be strengthened or more appropriately taught in other environments as well, including in programs run by the public sector. Furthermore, public policy has a role in defining, monitoring, regulating, and even providing socioemotional skills development, just has been the case for cognitive skills development.

Policy makers in the Philippines thus have a range of options on when in the schooling cycle to intervene to invest in the development of these skills. In the following review of international experience, these interventions are examined in three main stages: (i) before children start school—both home and center based, (ii) interventions at school both within the curricula and extracurricular, and (iii) interventions post school.

Review of International Experiences in Socioemotional Skills Development

Interventions in Early Childhood

Inequalities in early childhood development lead to an achievement gap that emerges even before preschool. Early childhood development programs have a high rate of return, and they often yield better outcomes than similar interventions later in life (Heckman, Stixrud, and Urzúa 2006). Although countries are increasingly adopting early childhood development programs to reduce inequality and promote academic and professional achievement, few of these programs have fully and explicitly incorporated socioemotional skills.

Because early childhood development programs target children who are not yet old enough to enroll in school, they typically take place in the home or in community centers. Home-based programs often focus on improving parenting practices and increasing the level of linguistic and cognitive stimulation provided by the home environment. Some home-based programs also include health services and/or nutritional support. These programs vary in terms of their length, intensity, and cost, which can range from US$500 to over US$4,500 per child per year (Sanchez Puerta, Valerio, and Bernal 2016). Home-based programs are especially well suited to reaching remote households and can be adapted to suit family schedules. Home visits offer the program provider a first-hand view of the child's home environment, which helps ensure that the program meets the child's specific needs (box 4.2).

Center-based programs typically provide a combination of education and stimulation services with nutrition at a community childcare center. Some programs are specifically designed to prepare children for school, whereas others focus on the child's overall developmental health and well-being. Although center-based programs do not necessarily enable providers to observe the child's home environment, they often provide childcare during the day, allowing parents to earn additional income. Center-based programs vary widely in terms of their staffing, resources, programmatic features, and cost, which can range from US$325 to US$13,400 per child per year (box 4.3) (Sanchez Puerta, Valerio, and Bernal 2016).

The international literature finds that early childhood development programs can prove highly cost-effective. Whether based in the home or in a community center, a well-designed and effectively targeted intervention can generate a dramatic improvement in cognitive and socioemotional skills. However, these interventions are best regarded as foundational, not comprehensive. Early childhood development lays the groundwork for the formation of cognitive and socioemotional skills, but most of those skills themselves are acquired later in life.

Box 4.2 The Jamaican Study Program

The Jamaican Study Program was a home-visiting program targeting children ages 9–24 months who lived in poor neighborhoods and whose growth had been stunted.[a] Participants were randomly assigned to one of four groups: (i) psychosocial stimulation, which consisted of weekly home visits with trained community health aides over a two-year period, with a curriculum that focused on language development, parenting skills, educational games, and activities to improve the self-esteem of both the child and the mother; (ii) nutritional supplementation, which consisting of 1 kilogram of milk formula provided each week for two years; (iii) both psychosocial stimulation and nutritional supplementation; and (iv) a control group.

The short-term outcomes of the program indicate that all three treatment groups experienced improvements in early cognitive development, but that psychosocial stimulation tended to be more effective than nutritional supplementation. Over the long term, only the psychosocial stimulation group experienced improvements in both cognitive and socioemotional skills, which increased the average earnings of participants at age 22 by 42 percent relative to the control group. These findings suggest that psychosocial stimulation can have substantial effects on labor market outcomes and may reduce economic inequality over time.

Source: Gertler et al. 2014; Sanchez Puerta, Valerio, and Bernal 2016.
a. Children who are clinically stunted are far below the median height for their age group. Stunting is often a sign of malnutrition.

Box 4.3 Save the Children's Early Childhood Development Program, Mozambique

Save the Children's Early Childhood Development Program seeks to promote the cognitive, social, emotional, and physical development of children in rural areas of Mozambique's remote and impoverished Gaza Province. It has two main components: (i) early stimulation, psychosocial support, and literacy and numeracy instruction in community-based preschool centers for three and a quarter hours every day; and (ii) monthly parenting meetings designed to enhance parenting techniques.

Communities are ultimately responsible for managing and sustaining the centers, which are staffed with volunteer teachers who are mentored, trained, and supervised by Save the Children. The program costs about US$2.50 per month per child. An evaluation of the program found significant increases in primary school enrollment, improvements in cognitive and problem-solving abilities, progress in motor skills, and better socioemotional and behavioral outcomes. However, the program did not have a measurable impact on language development, stunting, or wasting.

Source: Martinez, Nadeau, and Pereira 2012; Sanchez Puerta, Valerio, and Bernal 2016.

School-Based Interventions

Schools are the ideal environment in which to implement socioemotional development programs. These programs often teach a range of essential behavioral and life skills, such as the ability to solve conflicts, be assertive, and proactively manage aggressive or antisocial tendencies. Many school-based programs target at-risk youth and deal explicitly with issues such as crime, sexuality, and drug abuse. However, school-based socioemotional development programs can be immensely valuable to a wide range of children because they have been shown to increase engagement in education and improve test scores and grades. A positive classroom environment is associated with greater self-esteem, perceived cognitive competence, self-control, school satisfaction, academic performance, and positive behavior (Brown et al. 2010). As described in detail in the previous chapters, children with strong socioemotional skills are more likely to complete secondary school, pursue tertiary education, obtain employment, and earn higher wages.

Because core personality traits are in an ongoing formative process from childhood into late adulthood, school-based programs can provide continuous support for socioemotional skills development. Effective school-based programs can magnify the positive impact of earlier home- or center-based interventions, and they can help narrow the achievement gap between students from different socioeconomic backgrounds. School-based programs can enable providers to reach a large number of children without the need to arrange individual home visits or encourage parents to take their children to community centers, and a structured and supportive school environment can ease the implementation of socioemotional development programs (boxes 4.4 and 4.5).

Developing Socioemotional Skills for the Philippines' Labor Market
http://dx.doi.org/10.1596/978-1-4648-1191-3

Box 4.4 Schoolwide Positive Behavior Support, the United States

The U.S. Schoolwide Positive Behavior Support (SWPBS) model is a set of procedures and organizational systems designed to establish a school culture of positive behavior, with additional support for students with behavioral challenges. The SWPBS model is not a curriculum but a framework of school norms, practices for reinforcing positive behavior, and systems for data-driven decision making. The SWPBS model consists of three tiers of intervention. The first tier focuses on improving the overall school climate. Activities included in tier one include the following:

- *Defining and disseminating behavioral expectations for the school.* The school community selects school rules, and breaking these rules may trigger an individualized intervention.
- *Establishing rewards for appropriate behavior.* Students, teachers, administrators, and support staff are periodically rewarded for compliance with school rules. Rewards may be small, such as free entry to a school event or permission not to wear the required uniform to school for a day.
- *Creating a continuum of consequences for problem behavior.* This continuum allows problem behavior to be managed in a positive way that reflects the nature of the behavior itself. Group-based support is provided to help students manage both the social and academic aspects of school. Individualized behavioral assessments and skills-development programs are provided to students facing persistent challenges.
- *Implementing school-wide classroom-management practices.* Administrators ensure that the consequences of not adhering to school rules are widely known, and nonadherence is managed in a consistent manner across classrooms. By establishing consistent classroom-management practices, students are able to predict the consequences of their actions, and teachers spend less time managing problem behavior.

Randomized controlled trials show that the SWPBS model positively impacts student behavior. Horner et al. (2009) conducted a three-year study and found that the model decreased disciplinary problems and increased reading performance among third graders. Bradshaw, Mitchell, and Leaf (2010) conducted a five-year study and found that the SWPBS model significantly reduced problem behavior.

Source: Cunningham, Acosta, and Muller 2016.

Box 4.5 Building Socioemotional Skills in the Education System, Singapore and Mexico

Singapore, the top performer in the 2015 PISA, recently introduced a new comprehensive education model. Singaporean schools are broadening their focus beyond cognitive skills to incorporate character development and civic education, as part of a holistic approach to children's socioemotional well-being. The model, called "positive education," attempts to create a

box continues next page

Box 4.5 Building Socioemotional Skills in the Education System, Singapore and Mexico *(continued)*

scholastic culture that is supportive, caring, and trusting, and that directly links socioemotional well-being to academic excellence.

Mexico is also transforming its secondary education system to promote socioemotional skills development in adolescence. Mexico's *Construye-T* program targets students at the upper secondary level (grades 10–12). It trains teachers in classroom activities that promote socioemotional skills development. Analysis has revealed that this program positively affects education outcomes and can be implemented at a relatively low cost. Moreover, surveys indicate that Mexican employers regard many of the skills emphasized by the *Construye-T* program—such as teamwork, responsibility, and punctuality—as critical to productivity.

Source: Kattan 2017.

Because primary enrollment in the Philippines is close to universal, school-based socioemotional development programs would be able to reach children from all households in the country at a minimal administrative cost. Socioemotional skills can be taught like any other academic subject, such as math or reading. School-based programs leverage existing educational personnel and infrastructure, which enables them to be implemented at a low administrative cost and scaled up quickly. Unlike most home- or center-based early childhood development programs, school-based programs can be implemented nationwide, enabling them to reach children from all households.

A comprehensive approach to school-based socioemotional skills development requires training teachers, strengthening school policies, enhancing curricula, reorganizing class time, and investing in after-school programs. Training teachers in socioemotional skills can improve their effectiveness in the classrooms and enable them to model positive socioemotional skills for their students. School administrators can create an environment that is conducive to socioemotional skills development by defining and rewarding positive behaviors. Instruction in socioemotional skills can be integrated into the curriculum, and teachers can be taught to leverage pedagogical methods that support socioemotional skills development, such as interactive instruction, group learning, and collaborative problem solving. Schools should also set aside class time for teaching socioemotional skills. Extracurricular activities can enable students to practice and reinforce socioemotional skills beyond the classroom.

Teachers influence their students' socioemotional development in a variety of ways, and, without explicit instruction in socioemotional skills, teachers may not be aware of their profound impact on this aspect of their students' learning experience. Teachers' socioemotional skills affect how they interact with students, manage and organize their classrooms, and deal with problem behavior. Socioemotionally competent teachers are better able to manage their own emotions and create a well-structured environment that is conducive to their students' socioemotional development (boxes 4.6 and 4.7).

Teachers can integrate socioemotional skills development into classes designed to teach cognitive skills. Although socioemotional skills development is most closely associated with music, arts, physical education, and health classes, innovative pedagogical approaches can help enhance socioemotional skills in core academic subjects such as science and mathematics. This approach could be especially effective in the Philippines, where the school system devotes more time to core academic subjects than schools in many comparable countries.

Box 4.6 Best Practices for Training Teachers in Socioemotional Skills

Educational systems and schools should train teachers in techniques that have been shown to contribute to students' socioemotional development. Teacher training should include pedagogical methods designed to promote socioemotional skills, as well as instruction in the habits, attitudes, and values associated with strong socioemotional skills, because teachers continuously model these behaviors for their students even when teaching more traditional academic subjects. Teacher training should focus on the following:

- *Pedagogical techniques that reinforce socioemotional skills.* Learning exercises that require students to work together to plan, execute, and evaluate a task have been shown to strengthen socioemotional skills.
- *Positive socioemotional language.* Teachers can motivate students by using language that encourages hard work, reinforces positive behavior, or helps them visualize success through mental contrasting.
- *Improving teacher–student interactions.* Teachers must continuously demonstrate that they care about their students and are committed to treating them fairly.
- *Promoting cooperative learning.* Teachers can encourage students to study together and assist each other both in and outside the classroom.
- *Setting positive expectations and labeling appropriately.* The terms used to describe student performance can affect their self-confidence and encourage them to pursue further education. In the United States, replacing the label "proficient" with "advanced" on a state math exam significantly increased college attendance.
- *Improving classroom management.* Effective classroom management contributes to the development of both cognitive and socioemotional skills by reducing disruptions, fostering an environment conducive to learning, and maximizing the value of instructional time.
- *Encouraging teachers to model positive behavior.* Teachers who lack strong socioemotional skills model negative behaviors for their students. Instructing teachers in techniques to manage stress, maintain focus, reinforce self-control, and avoid negative behaviors such as tardiness and absenteeism can enable them to impart these skills to their students by serving as role models. Moreover, the international experience—though limited—indicates that teachers with higher socioemotional skill levels are more effective at teaching traditional academic subjects.

box continues next page

Box 4.6 Best Practices for Training Teachers in Socioemotional Skills *(continued)*

What Types of Practices Are Best Avoided?

Teaching can be, undoubtedly, one of the most stressful occupations because of the multiple emotional, pedagogical, managerial, and multitasking challenges it entails. Teacher stress and teacher burnout are negatively associated not only with the quality of the classroom learning environment and therefore with student performance but also with the quality of the teacher–child relationship and school engagement levels. Beyond their own stress, teachers' inability to cope with stressful situations in the classroom, or inactive behavior, may affect their capacity to manage student misbehavior.

Teacher behavior can also have a negative influence on students' socioemotional development. For example, if students or mentees perceive that their mentors will always bail them out from trouble, even well-intended mentoring can lower the perception of the cost of engaging in risky behaviors and therefore increase the incidence of these types of conducts. Teachers' (low) expectations about students' performance can also change students' perception of themselves and their behaviors according to the labels or expectations imposed on them. Another detrimental teacher behavior that might negatively affect students' socioemotional skills is teacher absenteeism/tardiness, although the evidence is more limited.

For teachers to be able to model and teach socioemotional skills, they themselves need to live and embody them. But this doesn't come to all teachers naturally. When teachers lack socioemotional skills, access to training, resources, creativity, or techniques to foster their students' socioemotional development, their behaviors and actions can produce negative learning outcomes. Existing evidence—which is still limited—suggests that training teachers to develop these skills can increase students' socioemotional (and academic) learning.

Source: Villaseñor 2017.

Box 4.7 Teacher Training in Socioemotional Skills Development, Peru

The Peruvian Ministry of Education's *Escuela Amiga* program is a year-long, university-level training course for teachers and school principals designed to develop participants' socioemotional skills and enhance their ability to create a school environment that fosters socioemotional skills development. The instructors are university psychology faculty, and the participants are primarily mid-career professionals. The course is designed to develop participants' empathy, tolerance, self-control, and decision-making skills; it also teaches methodologies for integrating socioemotional skills into classroom instruction. To ensure the course's relevance and practical applicability, participants' professional experiences are incorporated into the curriculum. After the course is completed, support teams regularly visit schools to provide follow-up.

The program has not yet been rigorously evaluated, but participant surveys suggest that the course enhanced participants' knowledge of socioemotional skills and how to use them in a scholastic setting. Ninety percent of participants felt that they were better able to manage

box continues next page

Box 4.7 Teacher Training in Socioemotional Skills Development, Peru *(continued)*

their classrooms, 93 percent believed that they were better equipped to manage conflicts at school, and 50 percent felt that their professional relationships had improved. Informal interviews with teachers and principals consistently indicated that the course's primary benefit was to promote better understanding of oneself, which enabled participants not only to perform better in the classroom but also to more effectively manage their children, marriages, and other personal and professional relationships. Participants often reported that they were initially reluctant to commit an entire year to the course but that, in retrospect, the benefits of the course more than justified the investment.

Source: Cunningham, Acosta, and Muller 2016.

Schools can also play a key role in promoting socioemotional skills development outside of normal school hours. Extracurricular programs conducted on school grounds can reach students who require additional attention or young people who are not enrolled in school. Many extracurricular programs involve sports, theater, arts, or technology; most programs directly incorporate socioemotional skills, often with the support of a trained specialist. Because of the extremely wide variety of extracurricular programs, the evidence regarding their effectiveness is mixed. Some programs targeting teenagers and young adults have had a statistically significant impact on employment and income, but the most effective extracurricular programs typically target younger students, especially young women in urban areas (box 4.8).

Postschool Interventions

Although socioemotional skills programs tend to be most effective in early and especially middle childhood, interventions targeting young people who have graduated or dropped out of school can have a significant positive impact on their socioemotional skills. Some postschool interventions focus on job placement; some attempt to reduce gender-based violence or improve participants' ability to cope with stress; and some aim to help participants overcome substance abuse or conduct disorders. Most postschool programs target unemployed or underemployed young people from poor and vulnerable households.

Most postschool socioemotional skills development programs attempt to either reintegrate former students back into the educational system or equip them with the competencies necessary to succeed in the labor market. These programs promote self-esteem, effective work habits, teamwork, positive negotiation and conflict-resolution techniques, time management and punctuality, professional appearance and body language, positive thinking, self-control, and stress management. Some programs offer technical training and teach job-search skills in addition to their socioemotional component. Socioemotional skills development can also be integrated into existing apprenticeship, internship, or job-training programs (box 4.9).

Box 4.8 Big Brothers and Big Sisters of America, the United States

Some extracurricular programs, like Big Brothers Big Sisters of America, target children who attend school and who have been referred to the program by school staff. Participating children are paired with a trained volunteer mentor who spends 45–60 minutes with the child about once a week. Although volunteers and children generally choose how they spend their time together, Big Brother Big Sister programs are often partially structured and in some cases activities predetermined. Activities rarely focus on academics but instead emphasize creativity and emotional openness. Arts and crafts, playing games, and talking about friends, family, school, and other personal issues are common activities in Big Brother Big Sister programs.

A randomized controlled trial involving 1,139 children in grades 4–9 found that the program had a significant positive impact on participants' (i) academic performance, (ii) confidence in their academic ability, (iii) college expectations, (iv) frequency of misconduct, (v) truancy, and (vi) dropout rates. However, no benefits were found in nonscholastic areas such as substance abuse, misconduct outside of school, relationships with parents and peers, social acceptance, self-esteem, and assertiveness. The program cost is estimated at US$1,000 per student per year.

Source: Herrera et al. 2008; Sanchez Puerta, Valerio, and Bernal 2016

Box 4.9 Postschool Interventions, the Dominican Republic

The Dominican Republic's *Juventud y Empleo* program is a workplace-based intervention that targets adolescents between the ages of 16 and 29 who live in poor neighborhoods, do not attend school, lack a high school diploma, and are unemployed, underemployed, or not participating in the labor force. The program provides 150 hours of vocational training, 75 hours of socioemotional skills training, and a three-month internship. Its objective is to help participants find a job, become well integrated into civil society, and avoid personally destructive and socially undesirable behaviors such as drug abuse and criminality. To facilitate participation, participants receive a stipend of just under US$3 per day.

The program has yielded significant positive results for both male and female participants. By 18–24 months after the intervention, job-quality indicators improved significantly among male participants—including a 17 percent increase in formal employment and a 7 percent increase in monthly earnings for employed workers—with especially positive effects in Santo Domingo. Among women, participation in the program is associated with lower rates of teenage pregnancy and improved expectations for the future. The program has measurably improved participants' leadership, persistence, and conflict-resolution skills. However, there is no measurable increase in the employment rate among participants.

box continues next page

Box 4.9 Postschool Interventions, the Dominican Republic *(continued)*

Six years after the intervention, improvement in job quality among male participants persists, with 25 percent more men in the treatment group having a job with health insurance, and with participants in Santo Domingo 30 percent more likely to have a job with health insurance. Participation in the program has also increased earnings among female participants in Santo Domingo by 25 percent over the control group.

Source: Ibarraran et al. 2014; Sanchez Puerta, Valerio, and Bernal 2016.

The Current State of Socioemotional Development Policy in the Philippines

The Philippine education and training sector has undergone significant reforms over the past decade designed to expand access to education and training services and improve their relevance and quality.[1] Public spending on education doubled in real terms between 2005 and 2015. In 2016, the government launched an ambitious program to extend compulsory education to encompass both kindergarten and upper secondary school. Enrollment rates have risen, and disparities in education access and quality have been slightly reduced. However, public spending on education in the Philippines remains relatively low by international standards, budget execution is poor, and the authorities have been slow to implement important reforms.

The Philippine education system suffers from limited resources. Although the constitution guarantees the right of every Filipino to access quality education at all levels,[2] resource constraints have forced the government to focus on kindergarten, elementary, and secondary school. Even at these levels, per-student funding is low by international standards, which reduces the quality of schools and constrains the supply of educational materials and qualified teachers. Consequently, student–teacher ratios at the elementary and secondary levels are higher in the Philippines than in other Association of Southeast Asian Nations countries as well as most lower-middle-income countries. Insufficient resources present a major obstacle to improving educational outcomes (Maligalig et al. 2010; Orbeta 2010; David and Albert 2012).

Evidence from the Philippines and comparable countries highlights the importance of investing in early childhood education and development (ECED). Although the Early Childhood Care and Development Act established a national ECED policy, its implementation is uncoordinated. The Department of Health implements health- and nutrition-related interventions targeting children under two years old; the Department of Social Welfare and Development provides day care and supplemental nutritional support for children three to five years old; and the Department of Education provides schooling and related services from kindergarten to grade 12. Previous efforts to establish a multisector approach to ECED yielded highly positive results but were not sustained over time. A renewed focus on coordinating ECED interventions could enhance their effectiveness (box 4.10).

Box 4.10 The Results of an Integrated Multisector Approach to ECED in the Philippines

In 1999, the Philippine government launched a five-year ECED project in the Western Visayas, Central Visayas, and Central Mindanao regions encompassing thirteen provinces and about 2.2 million households. In 2002, the project became part of the broader program encompassed by the Early Childhood Care and Development Act (Republic Act 8980). The program was designed to reduce infant mortality and support early childhood development, particularly among children from poor and vulnerable households by (i) minimizing health risks to very young children; (ii) increasing the knowledge of parents and the community regarding early child development and encouraging their active involvement in the development of children; (iii) advocating for child-friendly policies and legislation; (iv) building the capacity of child-related service providers; and (v) mobilizing resources and establishing sustainable financing mechanisms for ECED projects.

The program spanned a wide range of health, nutrition, education, and social services programs. The Department of Social Welfare and Development implemented the program in close coordination with the Department of Health, the Department of Education, and local government units. The program did not introduce new services but instead promoted an integrated, multisectoral approach to service delivery that included center-based and home-based interventions. To link the center-based and home-based services, the position of child development worker was established in all program areas. Child development workers assisted midwives and health workers in providing food and nutritional supplements, monitored children's health status, and provided ECED education to parents in the community.

At the municipal level, the program expanded nutritional support, parental education, and home-based day care programs. It also financed the construction of additional day care centers, upgrades to existing health facilities, and an increase in the supply of essential equipment and materials. The program trained service providers in areas including primary health care, parental education, case monitoring, growth monitoring, follow-up home visits, case referrals, and providing food and micronutrient supplements to children.

This approach generated impressive results across a range of child development indicators, especially among children who were involved in the program for more than 12 months. Cognitive, socioemotional, linguistic, and motor skills improved among participating children, with younger children exhibiting faster rates of improvement than older children. Unfortunately, the program was discontinued, and different institutions once again implement ECED programming without a formal coordination framework.

Source: Armecin et al. 2006.

In general, the Philippine public education curriculum devotes adequate instructional time to subjects that focus on developing cognitive skills. A total of 800 minutes of weekly instructional time is allocated to mathematics, science, and social studies at the elementary level, and 900 minutes are allocated at the secondary level. Philippine schools devote more time to these subjects than schools in Brunei Darussalam, Malaysia, and Singapore (figure 4.1) (Department

Figure 4.1 Instructional Time Allocated to Cognitive Skills, Philippines and Select Comparators

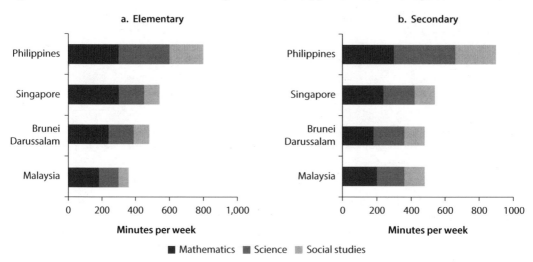

Source: Department of Education and SEAMEO INNOTECH 2012; World Bank calculations.

of Education and SEAMEO INNOTECH 2012). At the lower primary level (grades 1–3), the Philippine curriculum devotes 350 minutes per week to these subjects, more time than any of the other three countries. However, Malaysia and Singapore both outperform the Philippines in mathematics, which suggests that these countries may use their instructional time more efficiently.

The Philippine educational system allocates less time to subjects that foster the development of socioemotional skills than the education systems of peer countries. The elementary curriculum in particular devotes less time to music, arts, physical education, and health and values education than the curricula of comparable countries. The international evidence suggests that high-quality music and arts education can stimulate creativity, critical thinking, persistence, and motivation (Winner, Goldstein, and Vincent-Lancrin 2013). Similarly, physical education can support the development of social skills and self-esteem (Bailey 2006). The Philippine elementary schools allocate only 300 minutes per week to these subjects, less than elementary schools in Malaysia and Singapore and Malaysia, but the Philippine secondary schools devote more time to these subjects than secondary schools in other countries (figure 4.2).

Interviews with education sector officials revealed several reasons why the Philippine elementary education curriculum puts less emphasis on socioemotional skills than the curricula of other countries.[3] Interviewees described cognitive skills as being easier to measure and noted that instruments for measuring them are already in place. They also contended that the measurement of socioemotional skills can be influenced by local cultural factors, complicating comparisons between schools and regions. Moreover, under the current education policy, schools are judged by students' performance on tests that measure cognitive

Figure 4.2 Instructional Time Allocated to Socioemotional Skills Development, Philippines and Select Comparators

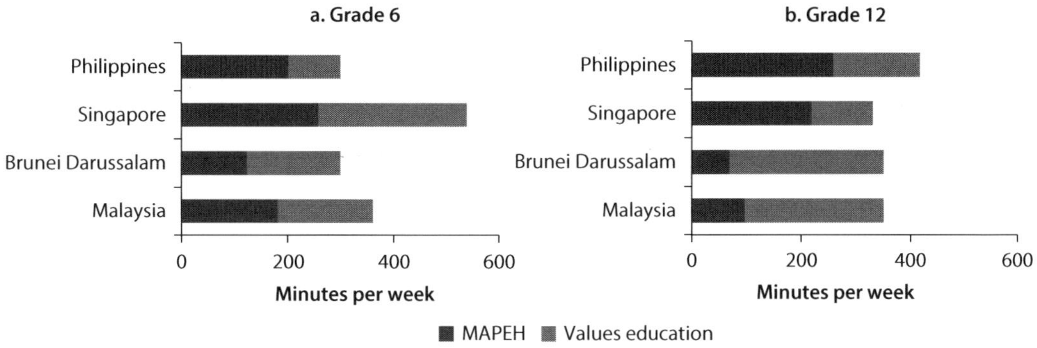

a. Grade 6   b. Grade 12

Minutes per week

■ MAPEH ■ Values education

Source: Department of Education and SEAMEO INNOTECH 2012; World Bank calculations.
Note: Refers to time allotment for grade 6 elementary and fourth-year secondary levels. MAPEH = music, arts, physical education, and health.

achievement, not socioemotional skills. Interviewees reported that teachers are not appropriately trained to develop socioemotional skills and that, with the country facing a high dropout rate, their priority is to focus on literacy and other core academic competencies.

Although the Philippine educational system has limited resources, cognitive and socioemotional skills development should not be viewed as rival subjects. Indeed, both national and international evidence suggests that developing students' socioemotional skills enhances their cognitive performance. A recent study on early childhood development in the Philippines, covering children from kindergarten to second grade, revealed that children with high socioemotional skill levels tend to achieve higher scores on literacy and mathematics tests (UNICEF 2017). Moreover, children who have attended preschool score higher on measures of both literacy and socioemotional skills, though not necessarily mathematics. As described earlier in this chapter, teachers can leverage pedagogical techniques to integrate socioemotional skills development into reading, math, and other core subjects without reducing the amount of time spent on those subjects.

Beyond instructional time, many other factors can limit socioemotional skills development. The UNICEF study cited above found that students taught by teachers with a master's degree and/or more than three years of preservice training tend to score much higher on measures of literacy, numeracy, and socioemotional skills. Children who have been exposed to conflict, a difficult home environment, and/or natural disasters tend to score much lower on measures of both cognitive and socioemotional skills.

For the postschool period, although apprenticeship-type programs exist in the Philippines, none has yet been properly evaluated to determine the impact on socioemotional skills. The Department of Labor and Employment (DOLE) is currently piloting a youth employment program known as JobStart, which includes a socioemotional development module. The result of the pilot will provide valuable information regarding its effect on employment and wages (box 4.11). Since the 1980s, the Technical Education and Skills Development Authority (TESDA) has been implementing a dual-training system model that combines classroom instruction with on-the-job training. Although it has been in place for several decades, the effect of the dual training system has only recently been evaluated, and preliminary results indicate positive effects on participant earnings (Yamauchi et al. 2017).

The Philippine government has recently launched initiatives to measure socio-emotional skills among job seekers. DOLE is testing new labor market information systems and tools, such as the TalentMap initiative to directly assess the competencies of job seekers to facilitate job matching (box 4.12). TalentMap is also being applied to the JobStart program to increase its retention rate and better match participants to prospective employers.

Increasing interagency coordination could enhance the effectiveness of job-matching and referral systems. DOLE's public employment offices should refer unsuccessful job seekers who require further skills development to the Department of Education's Alternative Learning System or the short-term training programs provided by TESDA. In turn, the Department of Education and TESDA should direct program graduates to DOLE employment offices rather than establish redundant job-matching systems.

Box 4.11 The JobStart Apprenticeship Program

The JobStart program is designed to facilitate the transition from school to work by enhancing the knowledge and skills of job seekers and enabling them to more effectively respond to the demands of the labor market. The program includes a "life skills training" module, which focuses on improving participants' socioemotional skills.

The initial JobStart pilot was implemented in 2014–15 and involved 1,600 participants in four municipalities. The program now reaches 3,600 participants but remains in its pilot phase. JobStart targets 18- to 24-year-olds who were at one point enrolled in secondary school, have no more than one year of work experience, and are not currently employed, enrolled in any other training, or actively seeking work. Participating firms employ JobStart trainees, who can account for no more than 20 percent of each firm's total workforce.

JobStart is currently being subjected to an impact evaluation. However, it has already reported a graduation rate of 67 percent, which is low by international standards, and a job placement rate among graduates of 75 percent. The addition of the TalentMap assessment module (box 4.12) is expected to raise both the graduation and job-placement rates by targeting especially promising participants and encouraging them to remain in the program.

Box 4.12 The TalentMap Initiative

The Philippine TalentMap© Initiative (PTMI) is a collaborative effort by DOLE, the SFI Group, and HireLabs to assess the skills and competencies of the country's workforce. The assessment is administered online through a series of questions that attempt to shed light on the job seeker's professional abilities and personal traits.

The assessment tool is intended to gauge not only cognitive and technical skills but also socioemotional skills. Although TalentMap can be used to facilitate job matching and program referrals at the individual level, its overarching objective is to provide detailed data on the skills profile of the Philippine workforce, enabling the authorities to design more effective education, training, and workforce development policies. TalentMap will ultimately be implemented in all DOLE employment offices, and all JobStart participants will be subject to the assessment. As of September 2017, TalentMap's pilot phase has involved nearly 30,000 participants in Metro Manila. The results of the pilot appear to confirm the findings of the STEP (Skills Toward Employability and Productivity) assessment: the largest skills gaps are in areas related to socioemotional skills, such as problem solving, innovation, decision making, planning and organization, teamwork, and problem sensitivity, rather than academic skills such as math and reading proficiency.

Notes

1. These reforms include the Kindergarten Education Act of 2012 (RA 10157), the Enhanced Basic Education Act of 2013 (RA 10533), the Ladderized Education Act of 2014 (RA 10647), and the Higher Education Reform Agenda.

2. 1987 Philippine Constitution Article XIV.

3. These interviews were conducted for this study and included officials from the Department of Education, the National Economic and Development Authority, the Commission on Higher Education, and the Technical Education and Skills Development Authority.

References

Armecin, Behrman, Duazo, Ghuman, Gultiano, King, and Lee. 2006. "Early Childhood Development through an Integrated Program: Evidence from the Philippines." Policy Research Working Paper 3922, World Bank, Washington, DC.

Bailey, Richard. 2006. "Physical Education and Sport in Schools: A Review of Benefits and Outcomes." *Journal of School Health* 76 (8): 397–401.

Bradshaw, Catherine P., Mary M. Mitchell, and Philip J. Leaf. 2010. "Examining the Effects of Schoolwide Positive Behavioral Interventions and Supports on Student Outcomes: Results from a Randomized Controlled Effectiveness Trial in Elementary Schools." *Journal of Positive Behavior Interventions* 12 (3): 133–48.

Brown, Joshua L., Stephanie M. Jones, Maria D. LaRusso, and J. Lawrence Aber. 2010. "Improving Classroom Quality: Teacher Influences and Experimental Impacts of the 4Rs Program." *Journal of Educational Psychology* 102 (1): 153–67.

Cunningham, Wendy, Pablo Acosta, and Noël Muller. 2016. *Minds and Behaviors at Work: Boosting Socioemotional Skills for Latin America's Workforce*. Directions in Development Series. Washington, DC: World Bank.

David, Clarissa C., and Jose Ramon G. Albert. 2012. "Primary Education: Barriers to Entry and Bottlenecks to Completion." Philippine Institute for Development Studies Discussion Paper Series 2012–07, Manila, Philippines.

Department of Education and SEAMEO INNOTECH (Southeast Asian Ministers of Education Organization Regional Centre for Educational Innovation and Technology). 2012. *K to 12 Education in Southeast Asia: Regional Comparison of the Structure, Content, Organization, and Adequacy of Basic Education*. Quezon City: Philippine Department of Education and Seameo Innotech. http://www.seameo-innotech.org/wp-content/uploads/2014/01/PolRes%20-%20K%20to%2012%20in%20SEA.pdf.

Gertler, Paul, James Heckman, Rodrigo Pinto, Arianna Zanolini, Christel Vermeersch, Susan Walker, Susan M. Chang, and Sally Grantham-McGregor. 2014. "Labor Market Returns to an Early Childhood Stimulation Intervention in Jamaica." *Science* 344 (6187): 998–1001.

Guerra, N., K. Modecki, and W. Cunningham. 2014. "Social-Emotional Skills Development across the Life Span: PRACTICE." Policy Research Working Paper 7123, World Bank, Washington, DC.

Heckman, James J., Jora Stixrud, and Sergio Urzúa. 2006. "The Effects of Cognitive and Noncognitive Abilities on Labor Market Outcomes and Social Behavior." *Journal of Labor Economics* 24 (3): 411–82.

Herrera, Carla, Tina J. Kauh, Siobhan M. Cooney, Jean Baldwin Grossman, and Jennifer McMaken. 2008. "High School Students as Mentors: Findings from the Big Brothers Big Sisters School-Based Mentoring Impact Study." Public/Private Ventures, Philadelphia.

Horner, Robert H., George Sugai, Keith Smolkowski, Lucille Eber, Jean Nakasato, Anne W. Todd, and Jody Esperanza. 2009. "A Randomized, Wait-List Controlled Effectiveness Trial Assessing School-Wide Positive Behavior Support in Elementary Schools." *Journal of Positive Behavior Interventions* 11 (3): 133–44.

Ibarraran, Pablo, Laura Ripani, Bibiana Taboada, Juan Miguel Villa, and Brigida Garcia. 2014. "Life Skills, Employability and Training for Disadvantaged Youth: Evidence from a Randomized Evaluation Design." *IZA Journal of Labor and Development* 3: 1–24.

Kattan, Raja Bentaouet. 2017. "Non-Cognitive Skills: What Are They and Why Should We Care?" *Education for Global Development* (blog), May 8. https://blogs.worldbank.org/education/non-cognitive-skills-what-are-they-and-why-should-we-care.

Maligalig, Dalisay S., Rhona B. Caoli-Rodriguez, Arturo Martinez, Jr., and Sining Cuevas. 2010. "Education Outcomes in the Philippines." ADB Economics Working Paper 199. Mandaluyong City: Asian Development Bank.

Martinez, Sebastian, Sophie Nadeau, and Vitor Pereira. 2012. "The Promise of Preschool in Africa: A Randomized Impact Evaluation of Early Childhood Development in Rural Mozambique." World Bank, Washington, DC.

Orbeta, Aniceto C. 2010. "Schooling Disparities: An Early Life Lever for Better (or Worse) Equity in the Future." The Filipino Child Policy Brief No. 6, Philippine Institute for Development Studies, Manila, Philippines.

UNICEF (United Nations Children's Fund). 2017. "Philippines Early Childhood Care and Development Longitudinal Study."

Villaseñor, Paula. 2017. "How Can Teachers Cultivate (or Hinder) Students' Socio-Emotional Skills? World Bank." *Let's Talk Development* (blog), June 13. http://blogs .worldbank.org/developmenttalk/how-can-teachers-cultivate-or-hinder-students -socio-emotional-skills.

Winner, Ellen, Thalia R. Goldstein, and Stéphan Vincent-Lancrin. 2013. *Art for Art's Sake? The Impact of Arts Education.* Paris: OECD Publishing.

Yamauchi, Futoshi, Taejong Kim, Kye Woo Lee, and Marites Tiongco. 2017. "The Impacts of On-the-Job Training on Labor Market Outcomes in the Dual Training System in the Philippines." Unpublished report.

CHAPTER 5

Conclusion and Recommendations

In recent decades, the Philippines has made great strides in improving educational outcomes, but a widening skills gap appears to be slowing the growth of some of the most dynamic industries and sectors. A mounting body of research shows that the quantity of education, as measured by years of school and proficiency scores in academic subjects, is not an adequate metric for human capital. Although cognitive skills, technical skills, and educational attainment are all important components of productivity, socioemotional skills are increasingly vital to meet the complex demands of a modern labor market.

This study has shown that higher levels of socioemotional skills are associated with improved labor market outcomes and educational attainment in the Philippines. This finding is consistent with emerging evidence from around the world, which shows that employers increasingly demand workers with cognitive, technical, and socioemotional skills. In light of the widening skills gap reported by Philippine employers, improving the socioemotional skills of the Philippine labor force could enhance economy-wide competitiveness and accelerate growth.

The socioemotional skills that are necessary for success in the labor market must be taught from early childhood through early adulthood, with a particular focus on middle childhood. Early childhood development profoundly shapes each person's cognitive and socioemotional potential, but not until middle childhood does the individual begin to learn the socioemotional skills most valued by the labor market. Adolescence is a key period for reinforcing and building upon the skills learned in middle childhood. Socioemotional skills development programming should continue through secondary school and should not be limited to at-risk youth. Schools are the ideal setting in which to teach these skills because, of any public institution, the school environment has greatest influence over children and teenagers.

The Philippine government can strengthen both its educational and labor force policies to encourage the development of socioemotional skills. Previous efforts to coordinate agencies involved in ECED yielded impressive results, and the government should reestablish a harmonized framework for ECED, which will help lay the groundwork for improved socioemotional skills development. The authorities should integrate socioemotional skills into the curriculum for its newly compulsory kindergarten-through-grade-12 educational system. Mainstreaming socioemotional skills includes both (i) setting aside greater time for subjects such as music, arts, physical education, health, and values education and (ii) training teachers in pedagogical techniques that embed the teaching of socioeconomic skills in traditional academic subjects such as reading and math. Socioemotional skills can be similarly embedded in technical and vocational training programs. Over the longer term, greater investment in monitoring and evaluation tools—including TalentMap, additional labor force surveys, and international skills assessment such as PISA and PIAAC—will help ensure that the government's skills-development policy adapts to meet the shifting demands of an evolving labor market.

The Philippines can learn from the emerging successful experiences in these areas. Table 5.1 summarizes interventions from the international experience that have proven effective in fostering the development of socioemotional skills.

Table 5.1 Potential Interventions on Socioemotional Skills Development Drawing from Global Experiences

Stage (age)	Description	Country (name of program example)	Relevant actors in the Philippines
Early childhood (0–5)	Psychosocial stimulation based on regular visits from community health workers to teach parenting skills and encourage mothers and children to interact in ways that develop socioemotional skills (like playing)	Jamaica (Supplementation Program)	DSWD, DepEd, DoH
	Provision of integrated early childhood education and development services through community-driven mechanisms in targeted poor communities	Indonesia (Early Childhood Education and Development)	DSWD
	Generation and implementation of standards and quality-assurance systems, and the institutionalization of early childhood education and development at the district and provincial levels		
	Full-day (10 hours/day) childcare, nutrition, and transportation year-round, from infancy to kindergarten (approximately 250 days per year)	United States (Carolina Abecedarian Project)	DSWD, DepEd, DoH
	Children's participation in interdepartmental programs on nutrition, health, early education, and social services programs to minimize the health risks to very young children	Philippines (Early Child Development [ECD] Program)	DSWD, DepEd, DoH
	Contributing to the knowledge of parents and the community about child development and encouraging their active involvement		
	Advocating for child-friendly policies and legislation		
	Improving the ability and attitude of child-related service providers		
	Mobilizing resources and establishing viable financing mechanisms for ECD projects		

table continues next page

Table 5.1 Potential Interventions on Socioemotional Skills Development Drawing from Global Experiences *(continued)*

Stage (age)	Description	Country (name of program example)	Relevant actors in the Philippines
	Preschool curriculum composed of singing, drawing, physical activities, vocabulary, and counting, designed for the 3-to-5-year age group	Cambodia (Preschool Program)	DSWD, DepEd
	Program combining (i) high-quality early stimulation, psychosocial support, and literacy and numeracy instruction in community-based preschool centers; and (ii) monthly parenting meetings oriented toward strengthening positive parenting practices. Communities ultimately responsible for managing and sustaining the centers, which are staffed with volunteer teachers who are mentored, trained, and supervised	Mozambique (Early Childhood Development Programme)	DSWD, DepEd
Elementary school (6–11)	School curricula with lessons of socioemotional skills (recognizing and understanding feelings, getting along with friends, emotional regulation, problem solving, and behavior at school). Lessons are reinforced by practicing skills after completing the structured curriculum, and continuing to practice the skills throughout the school day and at home. Program supplemented by parent training that focuses on positive discipline and engaging in their children's school lives via family homework.	United States, Western Europe (Incredible Years)	DepEd
	School norms and practices for reinforcing positive behavior, total school support (not just teachers), and data-driven decision making, consisting of improving school climate. Activities are implemented across the entire school to teach all students a set of behaviors.	United States (Schoolside Positive Behavior Support)	DepEd
	Comprehensive model of education looking beyond cognitive skills testing and incorporating character and citizenship education, with a holistic focus on children's socioemotional well-being and "development of the whole person." A "double helix" view of success that links socioemotional well-being with a focus on academic excellence.	Singapore (Positive Education)	DepEd
	Training of teachers and parents to promote parent–child attachment and teacher–child interactions. Elementary school teachers, receive training that includes proactive classroom management, interactive teaching, and cooperative learning. Parents are offered courses on behavioral management.	United States (Seattle Social Development Project)	DepEd
	Out-of-school programs using sports as the hook to attract participants and teach them cognitive and socioemotional skills. The rules of the games are changed in order to teach a range of socioemotional skills, including social problem solving, resilience, self-control, teamwork, initiative, confidence, and ethics. Children play on gender-mixed teams and are supported by mentors, who are trained to reinforce the socioemotional objectives of the program.	Colombia (Football with Heart)	DepEd

table continues next page

Table 5.1 Potential Interventions on Socioemotional Skills Development Drawing from Global Experiences *(continued)*

Stage (age)	Description	Country (name of program example)	Relevant actors in the Philippines
	Year-long training session, taught by university psychology staff, for mid-career teachers and school principals to develop their socioemotional skills so they can apply them in the classroom. The course is delivered through lectures, paper exercises, role-playing, and group interactions to recognize and manage a range of skills. The course incorporated real-time issues into the curricula, drawn from participants' work lives.	Peru (*Escuela Amiga*)	DepEd, CHED
Middle and high school (12–18)	Recruitment of graduates of elite colleges to teach in low-performing districts.	United States (Knowledge is Power Program)	DepEd, CHED
	Mentoring program in which volunteers have regular and lengthy one-on-one meetings with the enrollees for at least one year. This allows mentees and mentors to form stronger attachments and might help avoid the negative peer effects of grouping at-risk youth together.	United States (Big Brothers Big Sisters)	DepEd, CHED
	After-school one-on-one meetings with a trained staff member or meetings in small groups.	Portugal (Entrepreneurs for Social Inclusion)	DepEd
	Training of teachers and school principals, and distribution of toolkits of activities to develop socioemotional skills.	Mexico (*Construye T*)	DepEd
Adults (19+)	Training of skills involved in community improvement projects, while indirectly emphasizing improvements in social-emotional skills.	United States (Youthbuild)	DSWD, TESDA
	One-year center-based academic, vocational, and social skills training, including counseling. The program can also provide health services and a stipend during program enrollment.	United States (Job Corps)	TESDA, DOLE
	Classroom training, internship phase, and benefits. The socioemotional skills component includes a module of at least 75 hours (self-esteem and self-realization, communication, conflict resolution, life planning, time management, teamwork, decision making, hygiene and health, oversight, and job counseling).	Dominican Republic (*Juventud y Empleo*)	TESDA, DOLE
	Training course of 45 hours over nine days covering effective communication and business writing skills, team-building and teamwork skills (such as characteristics of a successful team, how to work in different roles within a team), time management, positive thinking and how to use it in business situations, excellence in providing customer service, and résumé and interviewing skills.	Jordan (New Opportunities for Women)	TESDA, DOLE
	Combination of (i) vocational (300 hours), academic (180 hours), and socioemotional skills (120 hours) training, delivered through a pedagogic method that uses arts and dance, and (ii) job placement services.	Brazil (Applause Warehouse)	TESDA, DOLE

table continues next page

Table 5.1 Potential Interventions on Socioemotional Skills Development Drawing from Global Experiences
(continued)

Stage (age)	Description	Country (name of program example)	Relevant actors in the Philippines
	Group course on cognitive behavior therapy focused on developing skills of self-control, such as the tendency to be playful, responsible, and resistant to temptation. The therapy also tries to foster a nonviolent, noncriminal self-image and set of values. The sessions employ a variety of techniques, from lectures and group discussions, to various forms of practice, including role playing in class, homework that requires practicing tasks, exposure to real situations, and in-class processing of experiences of executing these tasks.	Liberia (Sustainable Transformation of Youth)	TESDA, DOLE, DSWD

Source: Based on Sanchez Puerta, Valerio, and Bernal 2016.
Note: CHED = Commission of Higher Education; DepEd = Department of Education; DoH = Department of Health; DOLE = Department of Labor and Employment; DSWD = Department of Social Welfare and Development; TESDA = Technical Education and Skills Development Authority.

Reference

Sanchez Puerta, Maria Laura, Alexandria Valerio, and Marcela Gutierrez Bernal. 2016. *Taking Stock of Programs to Develop Sociomotional Skills.* Directions in Development Series. Washington, DC: World Bank.

APPENDIX A

Table A.1 Ordinary Least Squares Analysis of Labor Earning and Socioemotional Skills

Variable	(1)	(2)	(3)	(4)	(5)	(6)	(7)	(8)	(9)	(10)
Years of schooling	0.036***	0.034***	0.033***	0.033***	0.033***	0.034***	0.033***	0.034***		0.031***
	(0.006)	(0.006)	(0.006)	(0.006)	(0.006)	(0.006)	(0.006)	(0.006)		(0.006)
Reading skills used	0.097***	0.089**	0.091**	0.084**	0.084**	0.089**	0.080**	0.094***	0.119***	0.080**
	(0.036)	(0.036)	(0.036)	(0.036)	(0.036)	(0.036)	(0.036)	(0.036)	(0.036)	(0.037)
Complexity of numeracy skills used	0.077	0.086*	0.094*	0.088*	0.087*	0.087*	0.083	0.077	0.099*	0.084
	(0.051)	(0.052)	(0.052)	(0.052)	(0.052)	(0.052)	(0.051)	(0.051)	(0.053)	(0.052)
Agreeableness (standardized)		0.055							−0.096	−0.079
		(0.035)							(0.071)	(0.070)
Conscientiousness (standardized)			0.070**						0.065	0.038
			(0.035)						(0.058)	(0.058)
Decision making (standardized)				0.073**					0.044	0.040
				(0.036)					(0.065)	(0.064)
Extraversion (standardized)					0.089***				0.105	0.085
					(0.034)				(0.065)	(0.064)
Grit (standardized)						0.064*			−0.060	−0.053
						(0.037)			(0.080)	(0.079)
Openness to experience (standardized)							0.083**		0.058	0.053
							(0.033)		(0.071)	(0.070)
Emotional stability (standardized)								0.051*	0.028	0.014
								(0.030)	(0.038)	(0.038)
Constant	0.745**	0.837**	0.769**	0.914**	0.977***	0.841**	0.998***	0.688*	1.368***	1.008**
	(0.350)	(0.359)	(0.364)	(0.373)	(0.375)	(0.364)	(0.382)	(0.361)	(0.401)	(0.416)
Observations	1,351	1,350	1,351	1,351	1,351	1,351	1,351	1,351	1,350	1,350
R^2	0.193	0.195	0.196	0.197	0.198	0.196	0.197	0.195	0.183	0.200
Occupation dummy	Yes	Yes	Yes	Yes	Yes	Yes	Yes	Yes	Yes	Yes
Region dummy	Yes	Yes	Yes	Yes	Yes	Yes	Yes	Yes	Yes	Yes

Source: World Bank STEP Household Survey 2015; World Bank calculations.

Note: Robust standard errors are in parentheses. Conditional correlations are computed from the ordinary least squares. Ordinary least squares calculations control for being a woman, age, age squared, occupation, maternal education, and regions.

*** $p < 0.01$; ** $p < 0.05$; * $p < 0.1$.

Table A.2 Marginal Effect on Employment Probability and Socioemotional Skills

Variables	(1)	(2)	(3)	(4)	(5)	(6)	(7)	(8)	(9)	(10)
Years of schooling	0.005** (0.002)	-0.002 (0.002)	-0.003 (0.002)	-0.002 (0.002)	-0.002 (0.002)	-0.002 (0.002)	-0.002 (0.002)	-0.000 (0.002)	-0.003 (0.002)	-0.003 (0.002)
Reading skills used	-0.099*** (0.013)	-0.115*** (0.013)	-0.105*** (0.013)	-0.116*** (0.013)	-0.117*** (0.013)	-0.114*** (0.013)	-0.121*** (0.013)	-0.104*** (0.013)	-0.122*** (0.012)	-0.116*** (0.013)
Complexity of numeracy skills used	0.071*** (0.017)	0.088*** (0.016)	0.093*** (0.016)	0.089*** (0.017)	0.080*** (0.017)	0.086*** (0.016)	0.079*** (0.016)	0.075*** (0.016)	0.084*** (0.016)	0.087*** (0.016)
Agreeableness (standardized)		0.159*** (0.010)							0.056** (0.024)	0.055** (0.024)
Conscientiousness (standardized)			0.149*** (0.011)						0.019 (0.019)	0.023 (0.019)
Decision making (standardized)				0.150*** (0.010)					0.006 (0.023)	0.007 (0.023)
Extraversion (standardized)					0.147*** (0.011)				-0.011 (0.023)	-0.010 (0.023)
Grit (standardized)						0.156*** (0.010)			0.030 (0.027)	0.030 (0.027)
Openness to experience (standardized)							0.156*** (0.010)		0.051** (0.024)	0.051** (0.024)
Emotional stability (standardized)								0.124*** (0.011)	0.032** (0.015)	0.033** (0.015)
Observations	2,489	2,488	2,489	2,489	2,489	2,489	2,489	2,489	2,488	2,488
Region dummy	Yes	Yes	Yes	Yes	Yes	Yes	Yes	Yes	Yes	Yes

Source: World Bank STEP Household Survey 2015; World Bank calculations.

Note: Standard errors are in parentheses. Marginal effects on work probability are computed from a Probit estimation, taking into account standardized personality traits, being a woman, age, age squared, occupation, maternal education, and regions.

*** p < 0.01; ** p < 0.05.

Table A.3 Marginal Effect on Completion of Secondary Education and Socioemotional Skills

Variables	(1)	(2)	(3)	(4)	(5)	(6)	(7)	(8)	(9)
Reading skills used	0.195***	0.146***	0.150***	0.154***	0.169***	0.151***	0.148***	0.146***	0.147***
	(0.020)	(0.021)	(0.020)	(0.021)	(0.020)	(0.021)	(0.020)	(0.021)	(0.021)
Complexity of numeracy skills used	0.014	0.009	0.022	0.004	0.011	0.007	0.012	0.012	0.023
	(0.028)	(0.026)	(0.026)	(0.027)	(0.026)	(0.026)	(0.026)	(0.026)	(0.026)
Extraversion (standardized)		0.130***							0.023
		(0.015)							(0.036)
Conscientiousness (standardized)			0.170***						0.139***
			(0.016)						(0.032)
Openness to experience (standardized)				0.118***					-0.058*
				(0.016)					(0.035)
Emotional stability (standardized)					0.130***				0.040*
					(0.016)				(0.022)
Agreeableness (standardized)						0.134***			0.010
						(0.015)			(0.041)
Grit (standardized)							0.142***		0.002
							(0.015)		(0.043)
Decision making (standardized)								0.141***	0.031
								(0.015)	(0.036)
Observations	988	988	988	988	988	987	988	988	987
Region dummy	Yes	Yes	Yes	Yes	Yes	Yes	Yes	Yes	Yes
Above age 30	Yes	Yes	Yes	Yes	Yes	Yes	Yes	Yes	Yes

Source: World Bank STEP Household Survey 2015; World Bank calculations.

Note: Standard errors are in parentheses. Marginal effects on work probability are computed from a Probit estimation, taking into account standardized personality traits, being a woman, age, age-squared, occupation, maternal education, and regions.

*** $p < 0.01$; ** $p < 0.05$.

Table A.4 Marginal Effect on Pursuing Tertiary Education and Socioemotional Skills

Variables	(1)	(2)	(3)	(4)	(5)	(6)	(7)	(8)
Reading skills used	0.205***	0.214***	0.215***	0.225***	0.215***	0.212***	0.212***	0.209***
	(0.014)	(0.013)	(0.014)	(0.013)	(0.014)	(0.014)	(0.014)	(0.014)
Complexity of numeracy skills used	0.056*	0.067**	0.055*	0.059**	0.056*	0.059**	0.058**	0.067**
	(0.029)	(0.029)	(0.030)	(0.030)	(0.029)	(0.029)	(0.029)	(0.029)
Extraversion (standardized)	0.094***							0.092***
	(0.014)							(0.029)
Conscientiousness (standardized)		0.100***						0.097***
		(0.014)						(0.024)
Openness to experience (standardized)			0.069***					−0.023
			(0.014)					(0.029)
Emotional stability(standardized)				0.065***				0.014
				(0.014)				(0.019)
Agreeableness (standardized)					0.070***			−0.041
					(0.014)			(0.032)
Grit (standardized)						0.080***		−0.027
						(0.015)		(0.037)
Decision making (standardized)							0.078***	−0.001
							(0.015)	(0.031)
Observations	988	988	988	988	987	988	988	987
Occupation dummy	Yes	Yes	Yes	Yes	Yes	Yes	Yes	Yes
Region dummy	Yes	Yes	Yes	Yes	Yes	Yes	Yes	Yes
Above age 30	Yes	Yes	Yes	Yes	Yes	Yes	Yes	Yes

Source: World Bank STEP Household Survey 2015; World Bank calculations.

Note: Standard errors are in parentheses. Marginal effects on work probability are computed from a Probit estimation, taking into account standardized personality traits, being a woman, age, age squared, occupation, maternal education, and regions.

*** $p < 0.01$; ** $p < 0.05$; * $p < 0.1$.

Environmental Benefits Statement

The World Bank Group is committed to reducing its environmental footprint. In support of this commitment, we leverage electronic publishing options and print-on-demand technology, which is located in regional hubs worldwide. Together, these initiatives enable print runs to be lowered and shipping distances decreased, resulting in reduced paper consumption, chemical use, greenhouse gas emissions, and waste.

We follow the recommended standards for paper use set by the Green Press Initiative. The majority of our books are printed on Forest Stewardship Council (FSC)–certified paper, with nearly all containing 50–100 percent recycled content. The recycled fiber in our book paper is either unbleached or bleached using totally chlorine-free (TCF), processed chlorine–free (PCF), or enhanced elemental chlorine–free (EECF) processes.

More information about the Bank's environmental philosophy can be found at http://www.worldbank.org/corporateresponsibility.